Suicide: Prevention, Intervention, & Postvention

2nd Edition

Daniel W. Clark, Ph.D.
Denise J. Thompson, M.S.W.
Victor Welzant, Psy.D.

INTERNATIONAL CRITICAL INCIDENT STRESS FOUNDATION

© 2007 by the
International Critical Incident Stress Foundation, Inc.
3290 Pine Orchard Lane, Suite 106
Ellicott City, MD 21042
(410) 750-9600
(410) 750-9601 fax
www.icisf.org

100% of the proceeds from the sale of this of this workbook benefit the
International Critical Incident Stress Foundation, Inc.
A Non-Profit Foundation

Printed in the United States of America

ISBN 0-9765815-3-1

Preface

Did you know?

> Suicide is the 11th leading cause of death in America, the 3rd leading cause of death for our youth.
>
> Approximately 30,000 people in America and 1,000,000 worldwide commit suicide every year.
>
> Every 16 minutes, an American commits suicide, affecting at least six people intimately.
>
> The Surgeon General recently declared suicide a "serious public health problem," is suing a call to action to develop and implement a National Strategy for Suicide Prevention.

Suicide knows no boundaries, touching all ages, ethnic groups, genders, occupations, geographic areas, and socioeconomic statuses. Within these varied populations, however, certain individuals and groups are at higher risk for taking their own lives. People who are contemplating the act of suicide exhibit signs and symptoms that, if we are aware, can be detected and acted upon.

We believe that suicide prevention and intervention are everyone's responsibility. All of us are responsible to do what we can within our communities to reduce the risk of someone taking their own life. Awareness of the risk factors as well as signs and symptoms is a critical factor in effective suicide prevention.

A second factor is intervention, being willing to act on that awareness when you see someone who concerns you. Most suicidal behaviors can be prevented, if detected and acted upon early enough.

The final factor, postvention, addresses how we can best respond to suicide survivors, those who are left behind after the loss of a loved one or friend to suicide.

This workbook focuses on using crisis intervention techniques to help someone who may be considering suicide. It does not address long term therapy issues nor directly deal with the problems which may have led a person to consider suicide. Our focus in this course and workbook is on applying psychological first aid to assist the person in crisis.

Thank you for your interest in learning more about suicide. We hope that you can use this material as you work with individuals and groups who have been touched by suicide.

About the Authors

Daniel W. Clark, PhD is a licensed clinical psychologist currently working as the Washington State Patrol Department Psychologist. Prior to working for WSP, Dr. Clark worked in inpatient, outpatient, and community mental health settings for the U.S. Army. He is currently a Lieutenant Colonel in the U.S Army Reserves. A member of the International Critical Incident Stress Foundation, Inc. faculty since 1998 and a recognized trainer since 1996, he is also past President of the Washington Critical Incident Stress Management Network. Dr. Clark routinely presents on a variety of topics including workplace violence; suicide prevention, intervention, and postvention; critical incident stress management; peer support; death notification; time, anger, and stress management; coping with change, communication skills, and related topics.

Denise J. Thompson, M.S.W. is a Licensed Clinical Social Worker. She received a BSW from Wartburg College, a MSW from Florida State University and is a doctoral student at the University of Northern Iowa. Maj Thompson is currently Chief, Behavioral Health for the Air Force Reserve Command (AFRC) and is stationed at Robins Air Force Base in Warner Robins, GA. In her present position she is responsible for the implementation and oversight of the following AFRC programs: Suicide and Violence Prevention, Post-Suicide Review, Critical Incident Stress Management, and Operational and Post-deployment Stress. She has over 11 years of military service, including active duty and reserve service. Maj Thompson provides oversight and training for over 180 AFRC personnel, military and civilian, who are part of the AFRC CISM team. Prior to her current assignment with AFRC, she was in private practice providing services to adults and children who were affected by traumatic events, was a contract provider for the Veterans' Administration and was an Employees Assistance Program provider for the US Postal Service. Maj Thompson routinely presents on a variety of topics for military and civilian personnel regarding suicide prevention, intervention and postvention; workplace violence; critical incident stress management; and operational stress management. Maj Thompson is an approved instructor for the following courses: CISM: Basic, Individual Crisis Intervention and Peer Support; Suicide Prevention, Intervention and Postvention; and National Guard Trained Crisis Responder: Terrorism and Disaster Response.

Victor Welzant, Psy.D., is the Director of Education and Training, and faculty for the International Critical Incident Stress Foundation, Inc. Additionally, he serves as a consultant and Director of Acute Trauma Services for the Sheppard Pratt Health System in Towson, MD. Victor's other professional activities include serving as a consultant to the Maryland Mental Hygiene Administration in Disaster Behavioral Health and Trauma, and he is a member of the Maryland MHA Disaster Behavioral Health Advisory Committee. Victor is the Clinical Director of the Anne Arundel County Fire Department CISM Team, supervisor of the Sheppard Pratt Health System CISM team, and member of the Howard County CISM team in Maryland. Dr. Welzant is also in private practice in Towson MD, where he specializes in the treatment and supervision of Trauma and Stress related conditions. He serves as a consultant to the Baltimore County Police Department's Hostage Negotiation Team, and as adjunct faculty in Psychology and Nursing at Towson University. He is a member of the Central Maryland Chapter of the American Red Cross Disaster Mental Health Team, as well as a member of the American Foundation for Suicide Prevention, the American Trauma Society, and the American Psychological Association. Victor lectures and consults nationally on the topics of Critical Incident Stress Management, Crisis Intervention, Suicide, and the Treatment of trauma related syndromes.

Table of Contents

Note:

The contents of this workbook are provided as a set of general guidelines only. The course or workbook is not intended to be used as a self- help manual, nor as a substitute for psychotherapy or professional mental health guidance. When in doubt, always consult a licensed mental health professional. Similarly, this manual may not be used as a substitute for formal training, supervision, or field experience.

The content of this course may be emotionally distressing to some participants. Participants are encouraged to leave the training at any point should they find the material excessively distressing. The instructor will be available to participants during the training to discuss any adverse reactions to the course material, should this occur.

SECTION ONE

Introduction

Introduction

Suicide encompasses a variety of thoughts, behaviors, and actions. It is a continuum, running from the fleeting suicidal thought on one end to completed suicide on the other end.

Dr. Ed Shneidman, co-founder and co-director of the Los Angeles Suicide Prevention Center, defines suicide as "a conscious act of self-induced annihilation, best understood as a multidimensional malaise in a needful individual who defines an issue for which the suicide is perceived as the best solution."

Suicide is not a recent development. Suicides have been documented as far back in time as the Pharaohs of Egypt. Across time and cultures, many societies, but not all, have banned suicide, except in extraordinary circumstances such as times of war.

In Western culture, suicide was prohibited after Church leaders documented what they considered to be unacceptably high suicide rates. St. Augustine, in approximately 460 AD, declared that no one was to end their life in order to seek a better life after death. At approximately the same time, Roman law also outlawed suicide plus mandated that property belonging to the deceased was forfeited to the government if the cause of death was determined to be suicide. Laws making suicidal behavior a crime were repealed only very recently.

How pervasive, then, is the problem of suicide? The scope of the problem is much larger than most of us realize. According to the American Association of Suicidology, approximately 32,439 individuals completed the act of suicide within the United States in the year 2004. These are deaths which were determined to be suicides. Most of us will agree that we probably did not count every completed suicide. An error rate of just 10% raises the annual total deaths due to suicide to over 35,000.

However, this number does not account for those individuals who did not complete the act of suicide but engaged in behavior we label a gesture or an attempt. A suicide **gesture** is representative of the completed suicidal act. A 'finger gun' pointing to the head or an imaginary knife drawn across a wrist represent suicide as does swallowing a dozen pills (a non-lethal dose) in an attempt to drawn attention to their pain.

What differentiates a gesture from a suicide **attempt** is the intent of the individual. If their intent was to die, we call their action an attempt. The actual action they took is not as important as their intent. For instance, the adolescent who takes a dozen aspirin, believing they will die from that dose and intending to die, would be classified as an attempt, even though it was a non-lethal action.

If we calculate the non-fatal suicide attempts and gestures at approximately 100 non-fatal attempts/ gestures per 1 completed suicide, the annual number affected by suicide rises to 3.5 million.

But that still does not account for all those individuals who are affected by suicide every year. If we further assume that approximately six people are intimately affected by each of these suicidal behaviors, the total number of people affected in the US every year by suicide swells to over 24 million!

Thus, if we look at only the number of people who complete suicide every year, we are only seeing the tip of a very large iceberg. With this complete perspective, then, it is not surprising that the Surgeon General of the US declared suicide a public health problem in 1999, calling for the need to raise public awareness and the need for multifaceted approaches.

OBJECTIVES:

- Identify or list physical, emotional, and verbal warning signs of suicide as well as know how to ask "the question."
- Identify or list do's and do not's of successful suicide intervention.
- Identify or list probable feelings and reactions of suicide survivors.
- Identify or list useful helping strategies when working with suicide survivors.
- Identify appropriate interventions to apply when responding to a suicide.

Definition of Suicide

"Suicide is a conscious act of self-induced annihilation, best understood as a multidimensional malaise in a needful individual who defines an issue for which the suicide is perceived as the best solution."

Dr. Ed Shneidman, Suicide as Psychache, 1993

Definitions

- Suicidology
- Suicide by cop (victim precipitated homicide)
- PTSD
- CISM

Suicide Survivors

Family members and others who survive following the death of their loved one by suicide

Suicide survivors include spouses, significant others, parents, children, grandparents, aunts, uncles, cousins, lovers, friends, co-workers, classmates, etc.

Continuum of Suicidal Behaviors

- Ideation
- Gesture
- Attempt
- Completion

Annual Number of US suicides

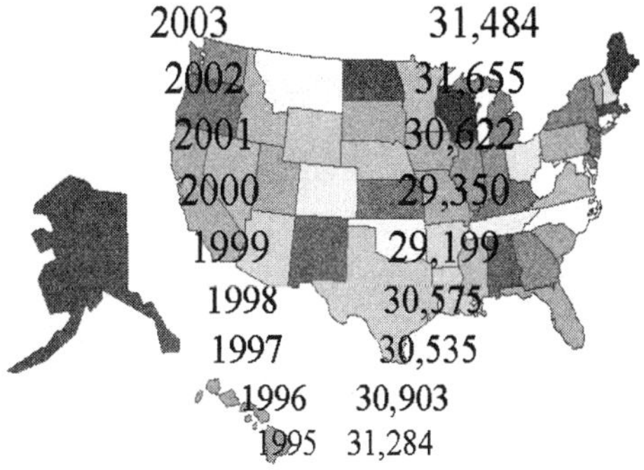

2004	32,439
2003	31,484
2002	31,655
2001	30,622
2000	29,350
1999	29,199
1998	30,575
1997	30,535
1996	30,903
1995	31,284

Startling Statistics
2004 data

- One suicide every 16.2 minutes
- 11th ranking cause of death in the US
- 811,000 suicide attempts every year
- 5 million living Americans have attempted suicide
- Each suicide affects at least 6 people intimately
- Firearms used in 52% of suicides

Frequency of US suicides

One

Suicide

every 16

minutes

Scope of the Problem

World Suicide Rates
WHO, 2002

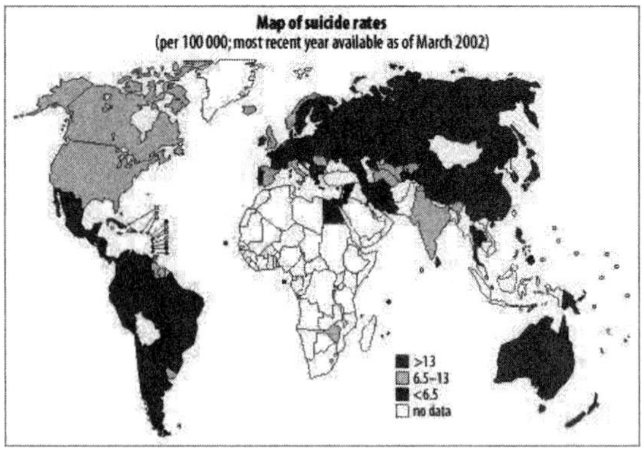

Suicide & Marital Status

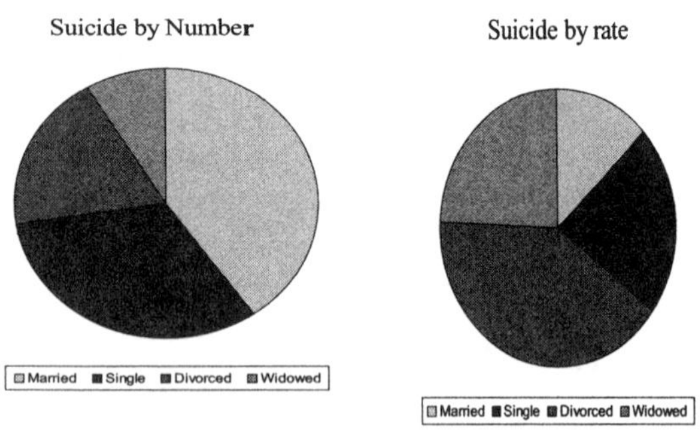

Suicide Demographics
Gender

Female:male ratio is 3:1 for **attempted** suicide

Female:male ratio is 1:4 for **completed** suicide

Methods of Suicide: by Gender, 2004 data

Method	Men percent	Men number	Women percent	Women number
Firearms	56.8%	14,523	32.4%	2,227
Hanging, strangulation, suffocation	23.4%	5,980	19.7%	1,356
Solid & liquid poisons	12.5%	3,200	37.8%	2,600
All other methods	7.3%	1,863	10.0%	690

Suicide Rates:

Gender, Race, & Age

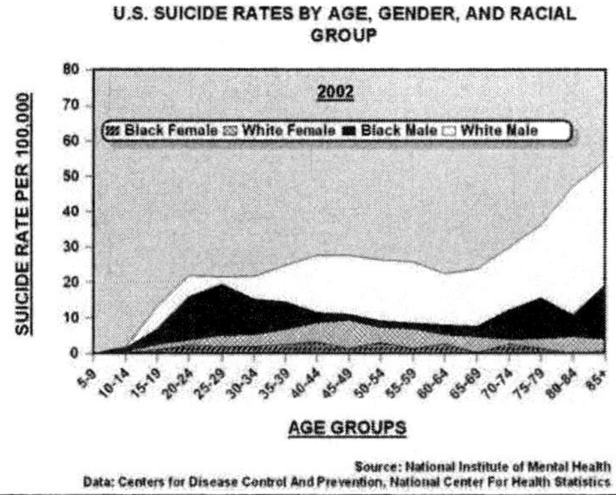

For More Information...

AAS
www.suicidology.org

J. McIntosh Statistics
mypage.iusb.edu/~jmcintos/

SAMHSA Suicide Prevention
www.mentalhealth.samhsa.gov/
suicideprevention

American Foundation for Suicide Prevention
www.afsp.org

U.S.A. SUICIDE: 2004 OFFICIAL FINAL DATA

	Number	Per Day	Rate	% of Deaths
Nation	32,439	88.6	11.1	1.4
Males	25,566	69.9	17.7	2.2
Females	6,873	18..8	4.6	0.6
Whites	29,251	79.9	12.3	1.4
Nonwhites	3,188	8.7	5.8	0.9
Blacks	2,019	5.5	5.2	0.7
Elderly (65+ yrs.)	5,198	14.2	14.3	0.3
Young (15-24 yrs.)	4,316	11.8	10.4	12.9

Group (Number of Suicides)	Rate
White Male (23,081)	19.6
White Female (6,170)	5.1
Nonwhite Male (2,485)	9.3
Nonwhite Female (703)	2.4
Black Male (1,655)	9.0
Black Female (364)	1.8
Hispanic (2,207)	5.3
Native Americans (404)	12.9
Asian/Pacific Islanders (765)	5.6

Completions: ***a slight increase from 2003 was seen in 2004, but pattern has primarily been stability or slight declines in recent years***

- Average of 1 person every 16.2 minutes killed themselves
- Average of 1 old person every 1 hour and 41.4 minutes killed themselves
- Average of 1 young person every 2 hours and 2.1 minutes killed themselves. (If the 285 suicides below age 15 are included, 1 young person every 1 hour and 54.5 minutes)
- 11th ranking cause of death in U.S.— 3rd for **young**------------------------------------>>
- 3.7 male deaths by suicide for each female death by suicide
- Suicide ranks 11th as a cause of death; Homicide ranks 15th

Cause	Number	Rate
All Causes	33,421	80.2
1-Accidents	15,449	37.1
2-Homicide	5,085	12.2
3-Suicide	4,316	10.4
10-14 yrs	283	1.3
15-19 yrs	1700	8.2
20-24 yrs	2616	12.5

Attempts (figures are estimates; no official U.S. national data are compiled):

- 811,000 [810,975] annual attempts in U.S. (using 25:1 ratio)
- 810,975 attempts translates to one attempt every 39 seconds
- 25 attempts for every death by suicide for nation; 100-200:1 for young; 4:1 for elderly
- 3 female attempts for each male attempt

Survivors (i.e., family members and friends of a loved one who died by suicide):

- *Each suicide intimately affects at least 6 other people* (estimate)
- Based on the 754,570 suicides from 1980 through 2004, estimated that the number of survivors of suicides in the U.S. is 4.5 million (1 of every 65 Americans in 2004); number grew by at least 194,634 in 2004
- If there is a suicide every 16.2 minutes, then there are 6 new survivors every 16.2 minutes as well

Suicide Methods	Number	Rate	Percent of Total		Number	Rate	Percent of Total
Firearm suicides	16,750	5.7	51.6%	All but Firearms	15,689	5.3	48.4%
Suffocation/Hanging	7,336	2.5	22.6%	Poisoning	5,800	2.0	17.9%
Cut/pierce	590	0.2	1.8%	Drowning	365	0.1	1.1%

U.S.A. Suicide Rates 1995-2004
(Rates per 100,000 population)

Group/ Age	1995	1996	1997	1998	1999	2000	2001	2002	2003	2004	Group/ Age
5-14	0.9	0.8	0.8	0.8	0.6	0.8	0.7	0.6	0.6	0.7	5-14
15-24	13.3	12.0	11.4	11.1	10.3	10.4	9.9	9.9	9.7	10.4	15-24
25-34	15.4	14.5	14.3	13.8	13.5	12.8	12.8	12.6	12.7	12.7	25-34
35-44	15.2	15.5	15.3	15.4	14.4	14.6	14.7	15.3	14.9	15.1	35-44
45-54	14.6	14.9	14.7	14.8	14.2	14.6	15.2	15.7	15.9	16.6	45-54
55-64	13.3	13.7	13.5	13.1	12.4	12.3	13.1	13.6	13.8	13.8	55-64
65-74	15.8	15.0	14.4	14.1	13.6	12.6	13.3	13.5	12.7	12.3	65-74
75-84	20.7	20.0	19.3	19.7	18.3	17.7	17.4	17.7	16.4	16.3	75-84
85+	21.6	20.2	20.8	21.0	19.2	19.4	17.5	18.0	16.9	16.4	85+
65+	18.1	17.3	16.8	16.9	15.9	15.3	15.3	15.6	14.6	14.3	65+
Total	11.9	11.6	11.4	11.3	10.7	10.7	10.8	11.0	10.8	11.1	Total
Men	19.8	19.3	18.7	18.6	17.6	17.5	17.6	17.9	17.6	17.7	Men
Women	4.4	4.4	4.4	4.4	4.1	4.1	4.1	4.3	4.3	4.6	Women
White	12.9	12.7	12.4	12.4	11.7	11.7	11.9	12.2	12.1	12.3	White
Nonwh	6.9	6.7	6.5	6.2	6.0	5.9	5.6	5.5	5.5	5.8	NonWh
Black	6.7	6.5	6.2	5.7	5.6	5.6	5.3	5.1	5.1	5.2	Black

15 Leading Causes of Death in the U.S.A., 2004
(total of 2,397,615 deaths; 816.5 rate)

Rank & Cause of Death	Rate	Deaths
1 Diseases of heart (heart disease)	222.2	652,486
2 Malignant neoplasms (cancer)	188.6	553,888
3 Cerebrovascular diseases (stroke)	51.1	150,074
4 Chronic lower respiratory diseases	41.5	121,987
5 Accidents (unintentional injuries)	38.1	112,012
6 Diabetes mellitus (diabetes)	24.9	73,138
7 Alzheimer's disease	22.5	65,965
8 Influenza & pneumonia	20.3	59,664
9 Nephritis, nephrosis (kidney disease)	14.5	42,480
10 Septicemia	11.4	33,373
11 Suicide [Intentional Self-Harm]	**11.1**	**32,439**
12 Chronic liver disease and cirrhosis	9.2	27,013
13 Essential hypertension and renal disease	7.9	23,076
14 Parkinson's disease	6.1	17,989
15 Homicide [Assault]	5.9	17,357
- All other causes (Residual)	141.2	414,674

Old made up 12.4% of 2004 population but represented 16.0% of the suicides.
Young were 14.2% of 2004 population and comprised 13.3% of the suicides.
972,264 Years of Potential Life Lost Before Age 75 (29,509 of 32,439 suicides below age 75)

Official data source: CDC's WISQARS website "Fatal Injury Reports" and "Leading Cause of Deaths Reports": http://www.cdc.gov/ncipc/wisqars/; obtained 12 Dec 2006

$$\text{suicide rate} = \frac{\text{number of suicides by group}}{\text{population of group}} \times 100{,}000$$

Suicide Data Page: 2004
15 December 2006
Prepared for *AAS* by John L. McIntosh, Ph.D.

Rate, Number, and Ranking of Suicide for Each U.S.A. State, 2004*

Rank	State [Division] (2003 rank)	Deaths	Rate
1	Alaska [P] (4)	155	23.6
2	Montana [M] (2)	175	18.9
2	Nevada [M] (3)	440	18.9
4	New Mexico [M] (5)	356	18.7
5	Wyoming [M] (1)	88	17.4
6	Colorado [M] (7)	797	17.3
7	Idaho [M] (8)	236	16.9
8	West Virginia [SA] (10)	285	15.7
9	Utah [M] (11)	377	15.6
10	Oregon [P] (6)	555	15.5
11	Arizona [M] (9)	880	15.3
12	Vermont [NE] (16T)	93	15.0
13	South Dakota [WNC] (16T)	112	14.5
14	Oklahoma [WSC] (14)	506	14.4
15	Florida [SA] (15)	2389	13.7
16	Kansas [WNC] (21)	370	13.5
16	Kentucky [ESC] (12)	560	13.5
18	Tennessee [ESC] (19)	792	13.4
18	Washington [P] (18)	830	13.4
20	Arkansas [WSC] (13)	361	13.1
21	Maine [NE] (36)	171	13.0
22	Missouri [WNC] (24T)	715	12.4
23	Mississippi [ESC] (27)	350	12.1
24	North Carolina [SA] (31)	1027	12.0
24	Wisconsin [ENC] (26)	662	12.0
24	Alabama [ESC] (28)	541	12.0
27	Louisiana [WSC] (38)	537	11.9
28	Iowa [WNC] (23)	343	11.6
29	Ohio [ENC] (43)	1319	11.5
29	South Carolina [SA] (29T)	482	11.5
29	North Dakota [WNC] (20)	73	11.5
32	Pennsylvania [MA] (34)	1410	11.4
33	Indiana [ENC] (24T)	704	11.3
34	Delaware [SA] (29T)	93	11.2
35	Virginia [SA] (33)	828	11.1
	Total	**32439**	**11.1**
36	Georgia [SA] (32)	973	10.9
36	Michigan [ENC] (39)	1098	10.9
38	Minnesota [WNC] (41)	524	10.3
39	New Hampshire [NE] (22)	133	10.2
39	Texas [WSC] (35)	2300	10.2
41	Nebraska [WNC] (40)	166	9.5
42	California [P] (42)	3368	9.4
43	Hawaii [P] (37)	116	9.2
44	Maryland [SA] (44)	500	9.0
45	Connecticut [NE] (46T)	294	8.4
46	Illinois [ENC] (45)	1028	8.1
47	Rhode Island [NE] (46T)	85	7.9
48	New Jersey [MA] (48)	597	6.9
49	Massachusetts [NE] (49)	425	6.6
50	New York [MA] (51)	1187	6.2
51	District of Columbia [SA] (50)	33	6.0

Caution: Annual fluctuations in state levels combined with often relatively small populations can make these data highly variable. The use of several years' data is preferable to conclusions based on single years alone.

Division [Abbreviation]	Rate	Number
Mountain [M]	16.9	3,349
East South Central [ESC]	12.8	2,243
South Atlantic [SA]	12.0	6,610
West North Central [WNC]	11.7	2,303
West South Central [WSC]	11.1	3,704
Nation	**11.1**	**32,439**
Pacific [P]	10.6	5,024
New England [NE]	8.4	1,201
East North Central [ENC]	8.1	4,811
Middle Atlantic [MA]	7.9	3,194

Region [Subdivision Abbreviations]	Rate	Number
West (M, P)	12.4	8,373
South (ESC, WSC, SA)	11.8	12,557
Nation	**11.1**	**32,439**
Midwest (WNC, ENC)	10.8	7,114
Northeast (NE, MA)	8.1	4,395

Source: CDC's WISQARS website and "Fatal Injury Reports": http://www.cdc.gov/ncipc/wisqars/ obtained 12 December 2006. [Note: divisional and regional figures calculated from state data] [data are by place of residence] [Suicide = ICD-10 Codes X60-X84, Y87.0]

Note: All rates are per 100,000 population.

* Including the District of Columbia.

Suicide State Data Page: 2004
16 December 2006

Prepared by John L. McIntosh, Ph.D. for

American Association of Suicidology

5221 Wisconsin Avenue, N.W.
Washington, DC 20015
(202) 237-2280

"to understand and prevent suicide as a means of promoting human well-being"

Visit the AAS website at:

http://www.suicidology.org

For other suicide data, and an archive of state data, visit the website below and click on the "Recent Suicide Statistics" link:

http://mypage.iusb.edu/~jmcintos/

NOTES

SECTION TWO

Prevention

Prevention

Suicide prevention has drawn national and international attention. Most industrialized countries have identified suicide as a public health issue. As it takes a village to raise a child, it takes a village to combat an act that has become insidious throughout society. Suicide knows no bounds, and as such, prevention programs must be prepared to address risk factors across a wide spectrum.

In response to suicide being identified as a public health issue, the National Strategy for Suicide Prevention (NSSP) was developed. The NSSP is a comprehensive public health initiative by the US Department of Health and Human Services and other government agencies. The NSSP aims to:

- prevent premature deaths due to suicide across the life span
- reduce the rates of other suicidal behavior
- reduce the harmful after-effects associated with suicidal behaviors and the traumatic impact of suicide on family and friends
- promote opportunities and settings to enhance resiliency, resourcefulness, respect and interconnectedness for individuals, families and communities

There are many population groups that are affected by suicide. Each group has unique risk factors and characteristics which should be included in a targeted prevention program. Age, race, and sex have been identified as potential risk factors. For 15-24 year olds, suicide was the 3rd leading cause of death. In 2000 more teenagers died from suicide than all medical conditions combined.

Individuals age 65 and older have the highest suicide rate of any age group. Individuals who are dealing with sexual orientation issues have a high rate of suicide attempts and suicidal thoughts. Males in every age group are more likely to complete suicide than females. Males choose a more lethal means than females. Divorced and widowed males commit suicide at a higher rate than males who are married. Females have more attempts per committed suicide and use less lethal means. Research also shows that within certain professions, the rate of suicide is higher than in others.

Protective factors of interconnectedness, social support and family support are essential in decreasing suicide. Increasing access to mental health and substance abuse services has been identified as a necessary part of a national plan to prevent suicide. Issues associated with increased access are destigmatizing and encouraging help-seeking behaviors.

Suicide prevention programs must be comprehensive in providing not only education regarding risk factors, but providing skills training to individuals at risk, training "gatekeepers" to identify individuals at risk, and creating services and increasing access to care so at-risk individuals can receive help when faced with what appears to be insurmountable and unmanageable pain. Individuals, organizations and communities have a responsibility to take part in prevention efforts. The end result is a healthier and more productive society.

Common myths about Suicide

- Happens without warning
- Low risk after mood improvement
- Once suicidal, always suicidal
- Intent on dying

- So rare, they won't do it
- Runs in the family
- No note ==> no suicide

Suicide Prevention: A Nation Responds

- 1999 "Surgeon General's Call to Action"
  - "Suicide is a serious public health problem"
- AIM
  - Awareness: Appropriately broaden the public's awareness of suicide and risk factors
  - Intervention: Enhance services and program, both population-based and clinical care
  - Methodology: Advance the science of suicide prevention

www.mentalhealth.org

Suicide Prevention: A Nation Responds

- National Strategy for Suicide Prevention
  - Implement 15 key recommendations from national conference in 1998
    - Recognized that mental health and substance abuse disorders confer the greatest risk for suicidal behavior
  - Public health model
  - Constructive public policy
  - Measurable overall objectives
  - Ways to monitor and evaluate progress
  - Provision of resources to carry out tasks

Principles of Suicide Prevention Programs

(Suicide Prevention: Prevention Effectiveness and Evaluation)

- Designed to enhance protective factors
  - Reverse or reduce known risk factors
- Long-term, continuous reinforcement of original prevention goals
- Family-focused programs may have greater impact that focusing on individuals
- Community programs are effective when combined with family-oriented strategies

Principles of Suicide Prevention Programs

(Suicide Prevention: Prevention Effectiveness and Evaluation)

- Emphasize, encourage help-seeking behavior
- Higher the risk of target population, more intense
- Be age-specific, developmentally appropriate and culturally sensitive
- Adapted to address specific nature of the problem in local community or population group

Organizational Suicide Prevention Programs

- Supported/endorsed by management & union
- Pamphlets, handouts, face-to-face briefings
  - "Self-Aid and Buddy Care" concept
  - Everyone has a responsibility
- Focus should be on identification of signs and signals, "red flags"
  - Depression
  - Self-destructive behavior
- Small/medium sized groups
  - Allows for questions and discussions
- Permeates organizational culture

Benefits of Dealing With Problems Early

- Prevent common stress reactions
- Address the issues while they are still manageable
- Prevent the "snowball effect"
- Prevent paper trail
- Eliminate consequences of seeking help
- Maintain quality-of-life and work productivity

Risk Factors

Patterson, W., et al, Psychosomatics, v24(4), 1983

- **S**ex (male)
- **A**ge (15-34) *(also 65+)*
- **D**epression
- **P**revious exposure to suicide
- **E**thanol/alcohol/drug abuse
- **R**ational thinking loss
- **S**ocial support system lacking
- **O**rganized plan
- **N**o spouse or significant other
- **S**ickness

Symptoms of Depression

DSM IV

- Change in sleep
- Change in appetite
- Loss of energy, motivation
- Loss of interest in pleasurable activity
- Feeling helpless, hopeless, apathy
- Deterioration of personal appearance
- Deterioration of job performance
- Frequent somatic complaints
- Preoccupation with death

Causes of Rational Thinking Loss

Lack of sleep

Stress or anxiety

Substance Abuse

Immaturity

Psychosis:

✦*Command hallucinations*

✦*Alien control*

✦*Religious preoccupation*

Social Support System

Warning signs

Separation from family or friends

- Geographic, legal, temporary

Loss of significant others

A loner or newcomer

Rejected by peers

Feels like people don't care

Life Events as Possible Triggers

- Suicide of loved one
- Death of loved one
- Serious family illness
- Loss of health
- Divorce/separation
- Divorce/remarriage of parents
- Loss of employment
- Loss of cherished possessions
- Retirement
- Financial problems
- Legal problems/Arrest
- Victim of crime
- Sexual abuse/assault
- Witness to violence
- Poor grades
- College rejections
- Sexuality concerns
- Physical abuse
- Substance abuse

Motivations for Suicide

Loss or change in an important relationship
To avoid or end perceived pain
Escape intolerable situation
Gain attention
Manipulate
Punish others/Punish self
Become a martyr

Direct Verbal Clues

I'm going to kill myself
I wish I were dead
You'd be better off without me
I might as well be dead
If …doesn't happen, I'm going to end it
I'm going to commit suicide

Indirect Verbal Clues

I can't go on any longer **I'm taking the plunge**
We all have to say goodbye sometime
Nobody needs me anymore **I'm tired of life**
You won't be seeing me any more
Life has lost meaning for me **I can't take it any more**
You'd be better off without me
I can't take the pain **Eat my gun**
You're going to regret how you treated me
Cash in my chips **Fold my hand**

Indirect Suicide Indicators

Clues.... Clues.... Clues....

- Buying a weapon
- Giving away possessions
- Making a will
- Talking about a long trip
- Taking unusual risks
- Changes in personality
- The "practice run"
- Sudden religious interest/ disinterest
- Substance abuse relapse

Major Predictors of Suicidal Behavior

How:

- Specificity of their plan
- Availability of means
- Lethality of method

History:

- A prior suicide attempt
- A family history of suicide behaviors

Help:

- Resources available

Specific indicators for special groups

Youth

Elderly

Military

Law Enforcement

PTSD

Substance Abuse

Youth Suicide
15-24 year olds

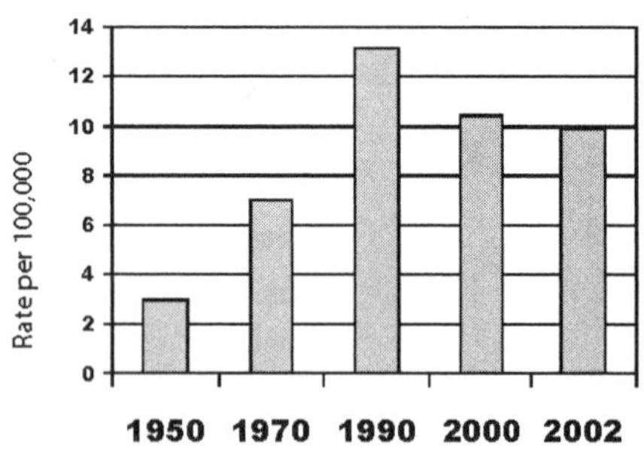

Youth Suicide

- 3rd leading cause of death among 15-24
- 1999 -- more teenagers and young adults died from suicide than cancer, heart disease, AIDS, birth defects, stroke and chronic lung disease
- Risk factors:
  - Depression, anxiety, disruptive behavior
  - Substance abuse
  - Family disruption, lack of family support
  - Increased availability of firearms
  - Previous attempt
  - Increased risk of suicidal behavior and thoughts in gay, lesbian or bisexual

Youth Suicide
2000 National Household Survey

- Based on 72,000 aged 12 and older plus 25,000 aged 14-17
  - Estimates 3 million youths at risk for suicide
  - 37% actually attempted
  - Suicide risk greater among 14–17, than 12-13
  - Suicide risk similar among Caucasian, African Americans, Hispanic and Asian youths
- Youths who reported alcohol or illicit drug use were more likely to be at risk
  - Illicit drug use other than marijuana (29%) were 3x more likely to be at risk than youths who did not use (10%)

Youth Suicide
Warning Signs

- Change in school attendance and/or performance
- Failure to complete assignments
- Talking or joking about suicide or death
- Increased risk-taking behaviors
- Substance abuse
- Wide mood swings, unexpected displays of emotion
- Impulsive behaviors
- Changes in appearance, personal care
- Changes in relationships
- Preoccupation with death or suicide

College Suicide

- 2d leading cause of death among college students
- Almost 1100 college suicides are projected to occur on campus each year
- Youth suicide rates vary widely among different racial and ethnic groups. Hispanics are at lowest risk and American Indians and Alaskan Natives are at highest risk.
- Seventy percent of youth who make a suicide attempt are frequent users of alcohol and/or other drugs.

College Suicide
Kisch, Leino, & Silverman (2005)

National College Health Assessment Survey

- 1.5% of college students reported suicide attempts
- 9.5% seriously considered suicide
- During the past school year,
  - 61.6% felt "hopeless" at least once
  - 33.4% reported experiencing "hopelessness" three or more times
  - 44.4% felt "so depressed it was difficult to function"
- Vulnerability higher in earlier college years
- Risk is lower than in matched non-college cohorts

Suicide Rates:

Age, Both Gender & All Races

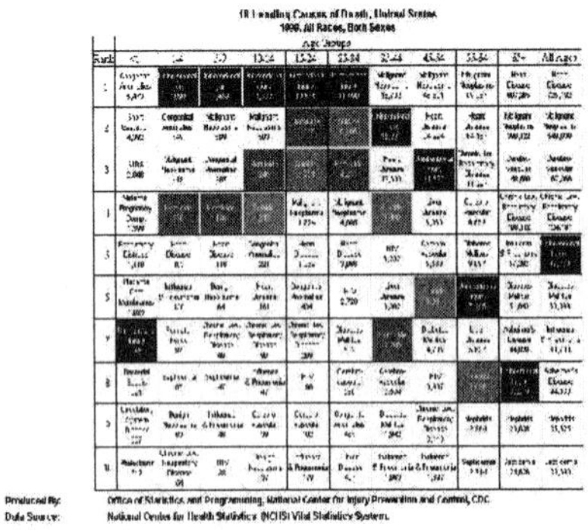

Suicide Rates:

Young & Old

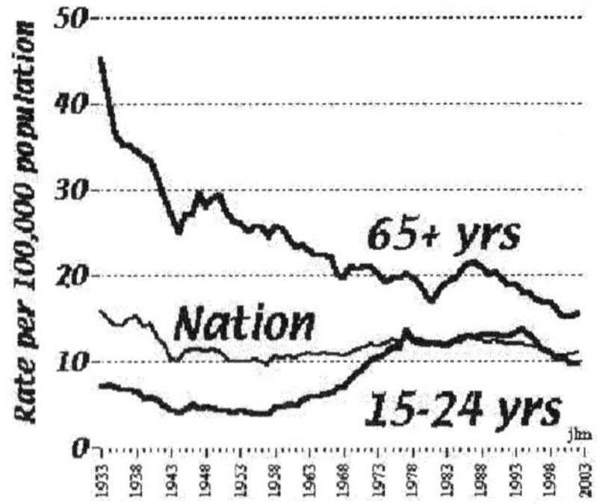

Source: http://mypage.iusb.edu/~jmcintos/SuicideStats.html

Elderly Suicide

- Suicide rates are highest among 65 and up
- 1 suicide every 90 minutes
  - 84 % of elderly suicide victims were male
- 13% of the population, 19% of all suicides
- Firearms (71%) most common method in 1998
  - Overdose (liquids, pills or gas) 11%
  - Suffocation 11%

Elderly Suicide

- Risk factors for elderly
  - Divorced men were 3.4 times and widowed men 2.6 times more likely than married men
  - Depression *(often undiagnosed – "normal")*
  - Increased physical illness, health care issues
  - Social isolation
  - Bereavement
  - Financial pressures
  - Substance abuse
  - Lethal means, less chance for intervention
  - Fewer attempts per completion

Elder* Suicide

Luoma, Martin & Pearson (2002)

- Primary care visits:
  - 58% one month prior to suicide
  - 77% one year prior to suicide
    - 100% women, 78% men
- Mental health visits:
  - 8.5% one year prior

* Age 55 and older

Military Suicide Rates

FY 1990-2004

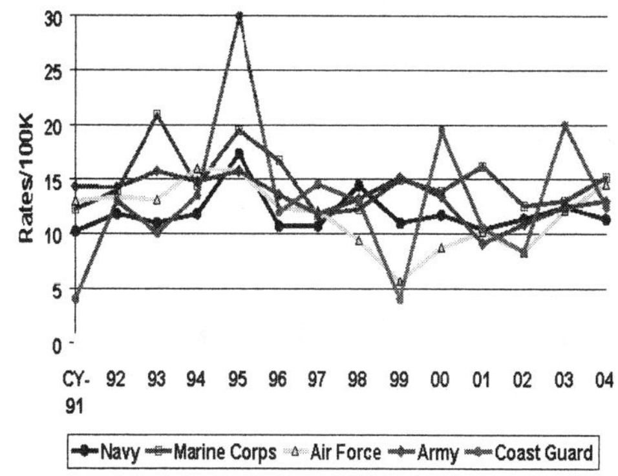

Military Suicides

Risk factors

- Difficulties in intimate relationships
- History of abuse, neglect, or rejection
- Depression
- Alcohol abuse
- Lower performance evaluations/work-related problems
- Military/legal problems
- Financial problems

Suicide in Specific Populations

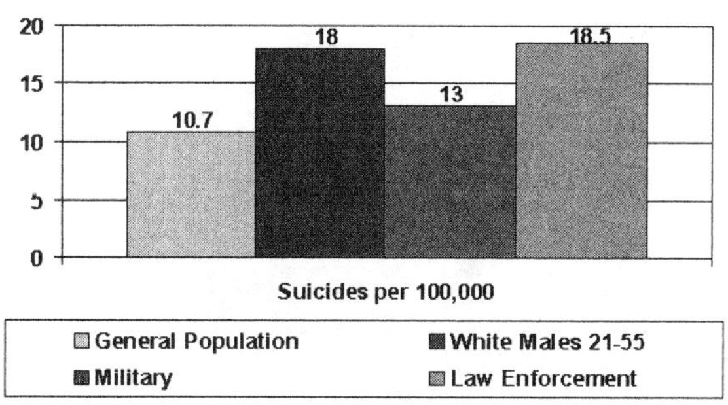

Law Enforcement Suicide

Janik & Kravitz (1994)

- Marital problems increases the risk of suicide 4.8 times
- Suspension increase the risk of suicide 6.7 times
- Marital problems **and** suspension combined increases the risk of suicide 21.7 times

Law Enforcement Suicide Compared to....

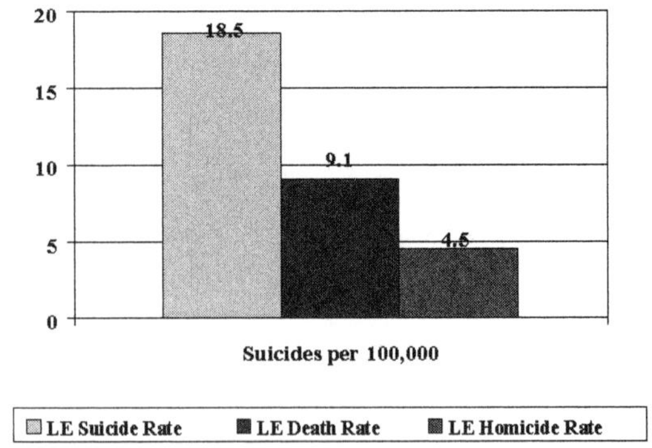

Law Enforcement Suicide and Retirement

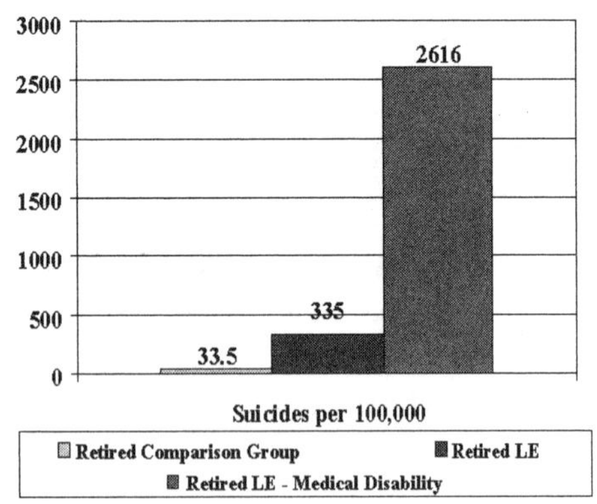

PTSD

Diagnostic criteria – DSM IV

- Exposure to a traumatic event
  - ➡ *(experienced/witnessed death/serious injury)*
- Persistently reexperienced
  - ➡ *(intrusive thoughts, dreams, flashbacks)*
- Avoidance of traumatic stimuli
  - ➡ *(forgets, anhedonia, shortened future)*
- Increased arousal symptoms
  - ➡ *(sleep changes, anger, hypervigilance)*

Suicide after Domestic Violence
(Thompson, Kaslow, et.al.,1999)

- Studied 119 women who recently attempted suicide
- Suicidal women were 3x more likely to report abuse and 3x more likely to meet criteria for PTSD than women with no history of suicidal behavior

Suicide and war trauma
(Bullman and Kang, 1996)

- Studied 4247 Vietnam Veterans with PTSD and 12,010 Veterans without PTSD
- Veterans with PTSD were 3.97X more likely to die from suicide (95% confidence interval)

Suicide and war trauma
(Hendin and Haas, 1991)

- Studied 100 veterans
- 19% made a post service suicide attempt
- An additional 15% reported being preoccupied with suicide since the war

Suicide and war trauma
(Hendin and Haas, 1991)

- Five factors were significantly related to suicide attempts:
  - Guilt about combat actions
  - Survivor guilt
  - Depression
  - Anxiety
  - Severe PTSD
- Combat guilt was most significant predictor of suicide attempts and preoccupation with suicide

Suicide after severe trauma
(Ferrada-Noli, Asberg, & Ormstad, 1998)

- Studied 65 refugees with PTSD and suicidal behavior
- Among those with PTSD, an association was found between the method of trauma (torture) and the method used in the suicide attempt or ideation

Suicide after severe trauma
(Ferrada-Noli, Asberg, & Ormstad, 1998)

- In 18 people subjected to blunt force trauma :
  - 14 (78%) reported jumping from a height or in front of a passing train as the content of SI
- In 6 people subjected to water torture:
  - 5 (83%) reported drowning as the content of SI
- In 5 people subjected to sharp force torture:
  - 3 (60%) reported cutting or stabbing as the content of SI
- In 3 cases of asphyctic torture:
  - 2 (66%) reported hanging as the content of SI

Suicide after natural disasters
(Krug, et. al, 1998)

- 7 year study of federally declared disasters
- 377 U.S. counties (19,453,900 residents)
- Suicide rates compared pre and post disaster AND to the U.S. base rate for suicide
- Controlled for multiple disaster exposure

Suicide after natural disasters
(Krug et. al, 1998)

- Demonstrated a statistically significant increase in suicide rates:
  - 13.8% in the 4 years following floods (308)
  - 31% in the 2 years following hurricanes (24)
  - 62.9% in the first year following earthquakes (4)

Suicide after Hurricane Katrina
New York Times, 27 DEC 05

- Preliminary data from Hurricane Katrina
  - 7 completions in 4 months
  - Population estimate of New Orleans 75-100K
  - Estimated rate = 21 to 28/100,000
  - Historical rate = 9/100,000

Suicide risk after terrorist acts: New York City
Galea et al. (NEJM, 2002)

- 1008 adults interviewed by phone (random digit dialing) between Oct. 16, 2001 and Nov. 15, 2001.
- 7.5% reported sx. consistent with dx. of PTSD
- 9.7% reported sx. consistent with dx. of depression
- Prevalence suggests that approx. 67,000 persons had PTSD and 87,000 persons were depressed at the time of the study

Suicide and Alcohol
(Gutheil,1999)

- Lifetime risk of suicide is 2-3x higher than the general population for those with alcoholism
- 15-25% of suicides are completed by those with alcoholism

Suicide and Alcohol

- Substance abuse
  - 50% rate of alcohol intoxication at time of death
  - 89% of suicide by alcoholics were actively drinking at time of death
  - Substance abuse associated with more frequent, repetitive, and mechanically lethal suicide attempts
  - Intoxication associated with disinhibition, increased impulsivity, and aggression

Suicide and Alcohol
(Canapary, Bongar, & Cleary, 2002)

- Medical seriousness of previous attempts
- History of suicide attempts
- Severe hopelessness

- Currently drinking
- Depressive episode
- Illicit drug use
- Living alone

Unique to alcohol

Suicide and Alcohol

Referral sources should be available

to address the issue of

substance abuse in order to reduce risk

AID LIFE

Ask - Don't be afraid to ask, "Are you thinking of hurting or killing yourself?"

Intervene immediately – Take action. Tell the person he or she is not alone.

Don't keep it a secret.

Locate help – Seek a mental health professional, peer supporter, chaplain, family member, friend.

Inform supervisor of the situation.

Find someone to stay with the person.

Expedite – Get help immediately. An at-risk person needs immediate attention.

Don't leave the person alone.

(Department/Company logo)

Suicide warning signs

Loss/change in important relationship
Expresses hopelessness, depression, guilt
Change in sleep and/or appetite
Minimal social support
Alcohol/Substance abuse
Legal problems/Financial problems
Under investigation
Talks about death or wanting to die

Resources

Mental Health Professional	xxx-xxxx
Chaplain	xxx-xxxx
Peer Support Team	xxx-xxxx
Employee Assistance	xxx-xxxx
Substance abuse counselor	xxx-xxxx
Suicide hotline	xxx-xxxx

AMERICAN ASSOCIATION OF SUICIDOLOGY

Dedicated to the Understanding and Prevention of Suicide

Suicide in the U.S.A.
Based on Current (2004) Statistics

1. In 2004 (the latest year for which we have national statistics), there were 32,439 suicides in the U.S. (89 suicides per day; 1 suicide every 16 minutes). This translates to an annual suicide rate of 11.5 per 100,000.

2. Suicide is the eleventh leading cause of death.

3. Suicide rates in the U.S. can best be characterized as mostly stable over time. Since 1990, rates have ranged between 12.4 and 10.7 per 100,000.

4. Rates of suicide are highest in the intermountain states. Eight of the 10 states with the highest suicide rates are from the intermountain region.

5. Males complete suicide at a rate four times that of females. However, females attempt suicide three times more often than males.

6. Relative to those younger, rates of completed suicide are highest among the elderly (age 80 and over).

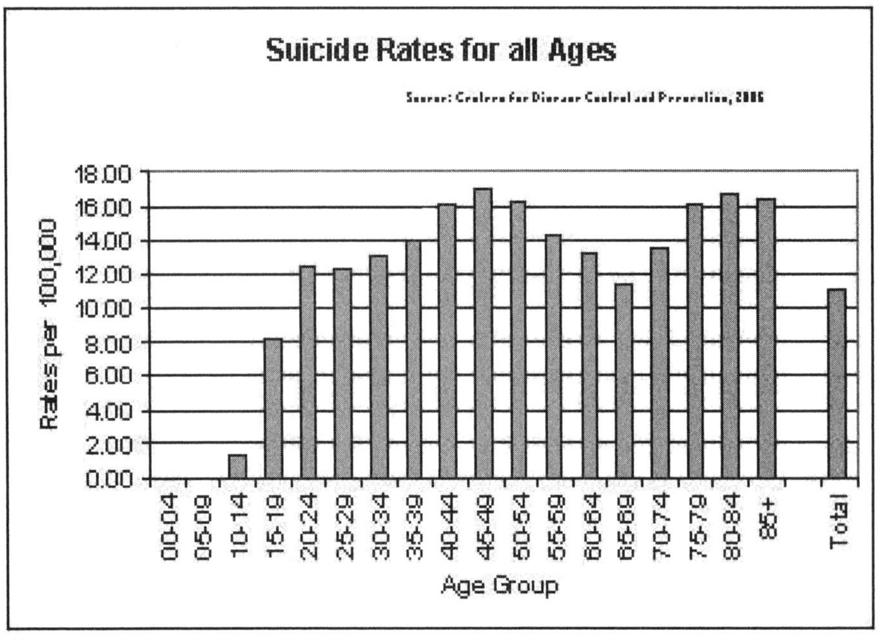

7. Elderly adults have rates of suicide close to 50% higher than that of the nation as a whole (all ages).

28 December 2006

8. Youth (ages 15-24) suicide rates increased more than 200% from the 1950's to the late 1970's. From the late 1970's to the mid 1990's, suicide rates for youth remained stable and, since then, have slightly decreased.

9. Suicide ranks third as a cause of death among young (15-24) Americans; only accidents and homicides occur more frequently.

10. Firearms remain the most commonly utilized method of completing suicide by essentially all groups. More than half (52%) of the individuals who took their own lives in 2004 used this method. Males (58% firearms; 42% other method) used firearms more often than their female counterparts (33% firearms; 67% other method).

11. The most common method of suicide for all females was poisoning. In fact, poisoning has surpassed firearms for female suicides since 2001.

12. Caucasians (12.3 per 100,000) have higher rates of completed suicides than African Americans (5.2 per 100,000).

13. Suicide rates have traditionally decreased in times of war and increased in times of economic crises.

14. Suicide rates are the highest among the divorced, separated, and widowed and lowest among the married.

Research Findings

- Although there are no official national statistics on attempted suicide (e.g., non-fatal actions) it is generally estimated that there are 25 attempts for each death by suicide.

- Risk of attempted (nonfatal) suicide is greatest among females and the young.

- Ratios of attempted to completed suicides for youth are estimated to range between 100 to 1 and 200 to 1.

- Mental health diagnoses are generally associated with a higher rate of suicide. Psychological autopsy studies reflect that more than 90% of completed suicides had one or more mental disorders.

- Those with the following diagnoses are at particular risk: depression, schizophrenia, drug and/or chemical dependency and conduct disorders (in adolescence).

- There is a relationship between depression and suicide; the risk of suicide is increased by more than 50 percent in depressed individuals. Aggregated research findings suggest that about 60 percent of suicides were depressed.

- There is a relationship between alcoholism and suicide; the risk of suicide in alcoholics is 50 to 70 percent higher than the general population.

- Feelings of hopelessness (e.g., there is no solution to my problem) are found to be more predictive of suicide risk than a diagnosis of depression per se.

- Socially isolated individuals are generally found to be at a higher risk for suicide.

- The vast majority of individuals who are suicidal often display cues and warning signs.

Warning Signs

Here's an Easy-to-Remember Mnemonic for the Warning Signs of Suicide: **IS PATH WARM?**

A person at risk for suicidal behavior most often will exhibit warning signs:

I	Ideation	→ Expressed or communicated ideation ○ Threatening to hurt or kill him/herself, or talking of wanting to hurt or kill him/herself; and/or ○ Looking for ways to kill him/herself by seeking access to firearms, available pills, or other means; and/or ○ Talking or writing about death, dying or suicide, when these actions are out of the ordinary.
S	Substance Abuse	→ Increased substance (alcohol or drug) use
P	Purposelessness	→ No reason for living; no sense of purpose in life
A	Anxiety	→ Anxiety, agitation, unable to sleep or sleeping all the time
T	Trapped	→ Feeling trapped (like there's no way out)
H	Hopelessness	→ Hopelessness
W	Withdrawal	→ Withdrawal from friends, family and society
A	Anger	→ Rage, uncontrolled anger, seeking revenge
R	Recklessness	→ Acting reckless or engaging in risk activities, seemingly without thinking
M	Mood Change	→ Dramatic mood changes

> These warning signs were derived as a consensus from a meeting of internationally-renowned clinical researchers held under the auspices of the AAS in Wellesley, MA in November 2003.

Other Issues

- The designation of "survivor of suicide" refers to the family members and friends who are impacted by the death of their loved one by suicide.

- Although the number of survivors is difficult to calculate, conservative estimates indicate that there are six survivors for every completed suicide. Based on data from 1980 to 2004, we can estimate that the number of survivors in the U.S. is approximately 4.5 million. An estimated 194,634 survivors of suicide were added in 2004.

Sources

The information for this fact sheet was gathered from the National Vital Statistics Reports on the National Center for Health Statistics website (http://www.cdc.gov/nchs/Default.htm) operated by the Center for Disease Control and Prevention. Unless specified otherwise, information presented refers to the latest available data (i.e. 2003).

American Association of Suicidology

The goal of the American Association of Suicidology (AAS) is to understand and prevent suicide. AAS promotes research, public awareness programs, education, and training for professionals, survivors, and all interested persons. AAS serves as a national clearinghouse for information on suicide. AAS has many resources and publications which are available to its membership and the general public. For membership information, please contact:

American Association for Suicidology
5221 Wisconsin Avenue, N. W.
Washington, D.C. 20015
Email: info@suicidology.org
Website: www.suicidology.org
(202) 237-2280 Fax: (202) 237-2282

AMERICAN ASSOCIATION OF SUICIDOLOGY

Dedicated to the Understanding and Prevention of Suicide

Facts about Suicide and Depression

FACTS ABOUT SUICIDE

In 2002, suicide was the eleventh leading cause of death in the U.S., claiming 31,655 lives. Suicide rates among youth (ages 15-24) have increased more than 200% in the last fifty years. The suicide rate is highest for the elderly (ages 65+) than for any other age group.

Four times more men than women complete suicide, but three times more women than men attempt suicide.

Suicide occurs across all ethnic, economic, social and age boundaries.

Many suicides are preventable. Most suicidal people desperately want to live; they are just unable to see alternatives to their problems. Most suicidal people give definite warning signals of their suicidal intentions, but those in close contact are often unaware of the significance of these warnings or unsure what to do about them.

Talking about suicide does not cause someone to become suicidal.

Surviving family members not only suffer the loss of a loved one to suicide, but are also themselves at higher risk for suicide and emotional problems.

WHAT IS DEPRESSION?

Major Depressive Disorder (MDD) is the most prevalent mental health disorder. In the U.S., the lifetime risk for MDD is 16.6% according to a recent study (Kessler et al., 2005). According to the National Institute of Mental Health (NIMH), 9.5-% or 18.8 million American adults suffer from a depressive illness in any given year.

The symptoms of depression (listed below) interfere with one's ability to function in all areas of life (work, family, sleep, etc).

Common symptoms of depression, reoccurring almost every day for a period of two weeks or more:

- Depressed mood (e.g. feeling sad or empty)
- Lack of interest in previously enjoyable activities
- Significant weight loss or gain, or decrease or increase in appetite
- Insomnia or hypersomnia
- Agitation, restlessness, irritability
- Fatigue or loss of energy
- Feelings of worthlessness, hopelessness, guilt
- Inability to think or concentrate, or indecisiveness
- Recurrent thoughts of death, recurrent suicidal ideation, suicide attempt or plan for completing suicide

June 10, 2005

A family history of depression (e.g., a parent) increases the chances (11-fold) that a child in that family will also have depression.

The treatment of depression is effective 60 to 80% of the time. However, according to the World Health Organization (WHO), less than 25% of individuals with depression receive adequate treatment.

Depression often is accompanied by co-morbid (co-occurring) mental disorders (such as alcohol or substance abuse) and, if left untreated, can lead to higher rates of recurrent episodes and higher rates of suicide.

THE LINK BETWEEN DEPRESSION AND SUICIDE

Suicide is the major life-threatening complication of depression.

Major Depressive Disorder (MDD) is the psychiatric diagnosis most commonly associated with completed suicide. Lifetime risk of suicide among patients with untreated MDD is nearly 20% (Gotlib & Hammen, 2002).

About 2/3 of people who complete suicide are depressed at the time of their deaths.

In a study conducted in Finland, of 71 individuals who completed suicide and who had Major Depressive Disorder, only 45% were receiving treatment at the time of death and only a third of these were taking antidepressants (Isometsa et al., 1994).

About 7 out of every 100 men and 1 out of every 100 women who have been diagnosed with depression at some time in their lifetime will go on to complete suicide.

The risk of suicide in people with Major Depressive Disorder is about 20 times that of the general population.

Individuals who have had multiple episodes of depression are at greater risk for suicide than those who have had one episode.

People who have a dependence on alcohol or drugs in addition to being depressed are at greater risk for suicide.

Individuals who are depressed and exhibit the following symptoms are at particular risk for suicide:

- Hopelessness
- Rage, uncontrolled anger, seeking revenge
- Acting reckless or engaging in risky activities, seemingly without thinking
- Feeling trapped – as if there's no way out
- Increasing alcohol or drug use
- Withdrawing from friends, family and society
- Anxiety, agitation, inability to sleep or sleeping all the time
- Dramatic mood changes
- Expressing no reason for living; no sense of purpose in life

TREATMENT

The most commonly used treatments for depression are:

- Pharmacology (i.e. antidepressants)
- Psychotherapy
- Electroconvulsive Therapy (ECT)

The best treatment for depression is the combination of antidepressants and psychotherapy. A meta-analysis of 16 studies (Pampallona et al., 2004) demonstrated the advantages of combined treatment versus pharmaceutical treatment alone. One hypothesis is that therapy increases adherence to the antidepressant treatment.

Treatments are effective 60 to 80% of the time. The Collaborative Depression Study indicates that after a first episode, 70% recovered within 5 years (National Institute of Mental Health).

In summary...

- Risk benefit ratio clearly resides on the side of treatment as opposed to no treatment for depression.
- The best treatment is combined pharmacology and psychotherapy.
- Most suicides in individuals with Major Depressive Disorder are among those who do not receive treatment.
- We still know too little about those who don't improve despite adequate treatment.
- More clinical research is needed.

ANTIDEPRESSANTS and SUICIDE RISK

In short-term studies, there has been some evidence that children and adolescents taking antidepressants exhibit a risk of increased suicidal ideation and/or suicidal behaviors (suicidality). Given this, the concern is that antidepressants could potentially lead to completed suicides.

The U.S. Food and Drug Administration (FDA) analyzed 24 trials that included over 4400 patients and concluded that the risk of suicidality in children and adolescents who were prescribed antidepressants was 4%, twice the placebo risk of 2% (www.fda.gov).

As with any new prescription in children and adolescents, careful monitoring of symptoms and side-effects should be observed by an adult. Any changes in symptomatology should be reported to the prescribing physician.

More research is required to determine if antidepressants are related to suicidality in children, adolescents and adults.

FDA 'BLACK BOX' WARNINGS

The Food and Drug Administration (FDA) is now requiring manufacturers of antidepressants to add a 'black box' warning label describing the potential risks of suicidality and the need for close monitoring of anyone prescribed this type of pharmacotherapy.

As well, the FDA developed a Patient Medication Guide (MedGuide), a user-friendly guide intended to educate patients and their caregivers about their prescription.
A joint meeting of the Psychopharmacologic Drugs Advisory Committee and the Pediatric Drugs Advisory Committee in September 2004 analyzed the short-term placebo-controlled trials of nine antidepressant drugs. The results demonstrated "a greater risk of suicidality during the first few months of treatment of those receiving antidepressants, the average risk of such events on drug was 4%, twice the placebo risk of 2%. No suicides occurred in these trials" (www.fda.gov). Based on these findings, the FDA issued the following warnings (the 'black box' warnings) regarding antidepressants:

- ☐ Antidepressants increase the risk of suicidal thinking and behavior (suicidality) in children and adolescents with MDD (Major Depressive Disorder) and other psychiatric disorders.
- ☐ Anyone considering the use of an antidepressant in a child or adolescent for any clinical use must balance the risk of increased suicidality with the clinical need.
- ☐ Patients who are started on therapy should be observed closely for clinical worsening, suicidality, or unusual changes in behavior.
- ☐ Families and caregivers should be advised to closely observe the patient and to communicate with the prescriber.

All patients being treated with antidepressants should be closely monitored for any changes in symptoms especially at the beginning of treatment or when the dose is adjusted up or down.

For more information on the FDA warnings, please visit their website (http://www.fda.gov/).

BE AWARE OF FEELINGS, THOUGHTS, AND BEHAVIORS

Nearly everyone at some time in his or her life thinks about suicide. Most everyone decides to live because they come to realize that the crisis they are experiencing is temporary, but death in not. On the other hand, people in the midst of a crisis often perceive their dilemma as inescapable and feel an utter loss of control. Frequently, they:

Can't stop the pain
Can't think clearly
Can't make decisions
Can't see any way out
Can't sleep, eat, or work
Can't get out of the depression
Can't make the sadness go away
Can't see the possibility of change
Can't see themselves as worthwhile
Can't get someone's attention
Can't seem to get control

If you experience any of these feelings, get help!

If you know someone who exhibits these feelings, offer help!

TALK TO SOMEONE -- YOU ARE NOT ALONE. CONTACT:

- A community mental health agency
- A school counselor or psychologist
- A suicide prevention/crisis intervention center
- A private therapist
- A family physician
- A religious/spiritual leader

American Association of Suicidology

The goal of the American Association of Suicidology (AAS) is to understand and prevent suicide. AAS promotes research, public awareness programs, education, and training for professionals, survivors, and all interested persons. AAS serves as a national clearinghouse for information on suicide. AAS has many resources and publications, which are available to its membership and the general public. For membership information, please contact:

American Association for Suicidology
5221 Wisconsin Avenue
Second Floor
Washington, D.C. 20015
Phone: (202) 237-2280
Fax: (202) 237-2282
Website: www.suicidology.org

References:

Gotlib, I. H. & Hammen, C. L. (Eds.). (2002). *Handbook of depression.* New York: Guilford Press.

Isometsa, E. T., Aro, H. M., Henriksson, M. M., Heikkinen, M. E., & Lonnquist, J. K. (1994). Suicide in major depression in different treatment settings. *Journal of Clinical Psychiatry, 55* (12), p. 523-527.

Kessler, E. C., Berglund, P., Demler, O., Jin, R., & Walters, E. E. (2005). Lifetime prevalence and age-of-onset distributions of DSM-IV disorders in the National Comorbidity Survey Replication. *Archives of General Psychiatry, 62*, p. 593.

Pampallona, S., Bollini, P., Tibaldi, G., Kupelnick, B., & Munizza, C. (2004). Combined pharmacotherapy and psychological treatment for depression: A systematic review. *Archives of General Psychiatry, 61* (7), p. 714-719.

Websites:

National Institute of Mental Health (http://www.nimh.nih.gov/)
U.S. Food & Drug Administration (http://www.fda.gov/)

AMERICAN ASSOCIATION OF SUICIDOLOGY
Dedicated to the Understanding and Prevention of Suicide

Youth[1] Suicide Fact Sheet

- In 2003, suicide ranked as the third leading cause of death for young people (ages 15-19 and 15-24); only accidents and homicides occurred more frequently.

- Whereas suicides accounted for 1.3% of all deaths in the U.S. annually, they comprised 11.9% of all deaths among 15-24 year olds.

> ○ Each year, there are approximately 10 youth suicides for every 100,000 youth.
> ○ Each day, there are approximately 11 youth suicides.
> ○ Every 2 hours and 11 minutes, a person under the age of 25 completes suicide.

- In 2003, 31,484 people completed suicide. Of these, 3,988 were completed by people between the ages of 15 and 24.

- Suicide rates, for 15-24 year olds, have more than doubled since the 1950's, and remained largely stable at these higher levels between the late 1970's and the mid 1990's. They have declined 28.5% since 1994.

- In the past 60 years, the suicide rate has quadrupled for males 15 to 24 years old, and has doubled for females of the same age (CDC, 2002).

- Suicide rates for those 15-19 years old increased 19% between 1980 and 1994. Since the peak in 1994 with 11.0 suicides per 100,000, there has been a 34% decrease. In 2003, the rate was 7.3 per 100,000.

- Males between the ages of 20 and 24 were 6 times more likely than females to complete suicide. Males between 15 and 19 were 4.4 times more likely than females to complete suicide (2003 data).

	Males	Females	Both genders
Ages 15 to 19	11.62	2.26	7.26
Ages 20 to 24	20.25	3.4	12.07

- For every completed suicide by youth, it is estimated that 100 to 200 attempts are made. Based on the 2003 Youth Risk Behavior Surveillance Survey, 8.5% of students in grades 9 through 12 reported

[1] In this fact sheet, youth refers to the age groups of 15 to 19 and 20 to 24. Unless otherwise specified, information presented refers to the latest available data (i.e., 2003).

12 February 2006

making an attempt at suicide in the previous 12 months (11.5% female and 5.4% male). These percentages decreased from grades 9 (10.1%) to 12 (6.1%). A prior suicide attempt is an important risk factor for an eventual completion. In fact, according to the YRBSS, 16.9% of students seriously considered attempting suicide in the previous 12 months and 16.5% of students made plans for an attempt (2003).

- Firearms remain the most commonly used suicide method among youth, accounting for 52% of all completed suicides.

- In the last decade, for youths aged 15 to 19, the suicide rate by firearm decreased (from 7.3 in 1992 to 3.7 in 2002); correspondingly, suicide rates by suffocation increased (from 1.9 in 1992 to 2.7 in 2002). Firearms remain the most commonly used method.

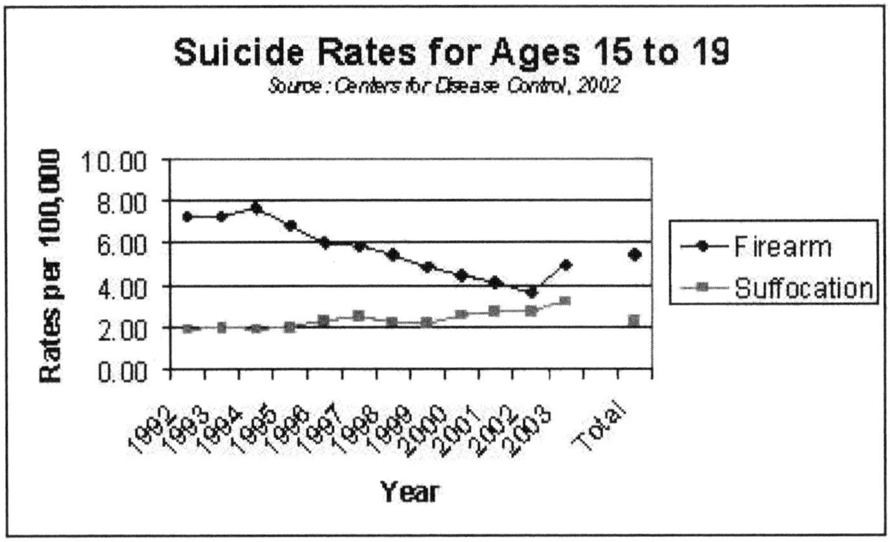

- Research has shown that the access to and the availability of firearms is a significant factor in observed increases in rates of youth suicide. Guns in the home are deadly to its occupants!

Suicide Among Children

- In 2003, 244 children ages 10 to 14 completed suicide in the U.S.

- Suicide rates for those between the ages of 10-14 increased 99% between 1980 and 1997. This age group has shown a 21% decrease since 1997. For 2003, the rate is 1.15 per 100,000.

- Although their rates are lower than for Caucasian youth, African American youth (ages 10-14) showed the largest increase in suicide rates between 1980 and 1995 (233%). The rate for African American males ages 10-14 was 1.88 per 100,000 in 2003.

- In the 10 to 14 age group, Caucasian youths (ranked 3rd leading cause of death) were far more likely to complete suicide than African American youths (ranked 5th leading cause of death). Caucasian males between 10 and 14 years of age were 3.4 times more likely to complete suicide than Caucasian females of the same age.

- The trend of methods used by children has followed a similar pattern to that of youths 15 to 19 years old. Since 1992, suicide by firearm decreased and suicide by suffocation increased. Suicides by suffocation among 10 to 14 year olds have occurred more frequently than those by firearms since 1999.

Other factors

- Research has shown that most adolescent suicides occur after school hours and in the teen's home.

- Although rates vary somewhat by geographic location, within a typical high school classroom, it is likely that three students (one boy and two girls) have made a suicide attempt in the past year.

- The typical profile of an adolescent nonfatal suicide attempter is a female who ingests pills, while the profile of the typical completer suicide is a male who dies from a gunshot wound.

- Not all adolescent attempters may admit their intent. Therefore, any deliberate self-harming behaviors should be considered serious and in need of further evaluation.

- *Most* adolescent suicide attempts are precipitated by interpersonal conflicts. The intent of the behavior appears to be to effect change in the behaviors or attitudes of others.

- Repeat attempters (those making more than one nonfatal attempt) generally use their behavior as a means of coping with stress and tend to exhibit more chronic symptomology, poorer coping histories, and a higher presence of suicidal and substance abusive behaviors in their family histories.

- Many teenagers may display one or more of the problems or "signs" detailed below. The following list describes some potential factors of risk for suicide among youth. If observed, a professional evaluation is strongly recommended:

    Presence of a psychiatric disorder (e.g., depression, drug or alcohol, behavior disorders, conduct disorder [e.g., runs away or has been incarcerated]);

    The expression/communication of thoughts of suicide, death, dying or the afterlife (in a context of sadness, boredom, hopelessness or negative feelings);

    Impulsive and aggressive behavior, frequent expressions of rage;

    Increasing use of alcohol or drugs;

    Exposure to another's suicidal behavior;

    Recent severe stressor (e.g., difficulties in dealing with sexual orientation; unplanned pregnancy, significant real or anticipated loss, etc.); and/or

    Family instability, significant family conflict.

Sources

The information for this portion of the fact sheet was gathered from the National Center for Injury Prevention and Control (NCIPC) website (www.cdc.gov/ncipc/wisqars/default.htm), a division of the Center for Disease Control and Prevention (CDC), and the Morbidity and Mortality Weekly Reports (May 21, 2004, 53 (SS-2); June 11, 2004, 53(4), p. 471-474).

Suicide Among College Students

- The rate of completed suicide for college students, according to a major study of suicides on Big Ten college campuses (1997) was 7.5 per 100,000.

- It is estimated that there are more than 1,000 suicides on college campuses per year.

- One in 12 college students have made a suicide plan.

- In 2000, the American College Health Association surveyed 16,000 college students from 28 college campuses.
    - 9.5% of students had seriously contemplated suicide.
    - 1.5% have made a suicide attempt.
    - In the twelve month period prior to the survey, half of the sample reported feeling very sad, one third reported feeling hopeless and 22% reported feeling so depressed as to not be able to function.
    - Of the 16,000 students surveyed, only 6.2% of males and 12.8% of females reported a diagnosis of depression. Therefore, there are a large number of students who are not receiving adequate treatment and/or who remain undiagnosed.

- Of the students who had seriously considered suicide, 94.8% reported feeling so sad to the point of not functioning at least once in the past year, and 94.4% reported feelings of hopelessness.

- Two groups of students might be at higher risk for suicide:
  - Students with a pre-existing (before college) mental health condition, and
  - Students who develop a mental health condition while in college.

  Within these groups, students who are male, Asian and Hispanic, under the age of 21 are more likely to experience suicide ideation and attempts.

- Reasons attributed to the appearance or increase of symptoms/disorders:
    - New and unfamiliar environment;
    - Academic and social pressures;
    - Feelings of failure or decreased performance;
    - Alienation;
    - Family history of mental illness;
    - Lack adequate coping skills;
    - Difficulties adjusting to new demands and different work loads.

- Risk factors for suicide in college students include depression, sadness, hopelessness, and stress.

- As with the general population, depression plays a large role in suicide. "Ten percent of college students have been diagnosed with depression" (NMHA, 2001). "The vast majority of young adults aged 18 and older who are diagnosed with depression do not receive appropriate or even any treatment at all".

Sources

The information for this portion of the fact sheet was gathered from:

Safeguarding your Students Against Suicide - Expanding the Safety Net: Proceedings from an Expert panel an Vulnerability, Depressive Symptoms, and Suicidal Behavior on College Campuses (2002), a report co-sponsored by the National Mental Health Association (NMHA) and the Jed Foundation.

Suicide Prevention Resource Center. (2004). *Promoting Mental Health and Preventing Suicide in College and University Settings*. Newton, MA: Education Development Center, Inc.

The Jed Foundation and the National Mental Health Association websites.

American Association of Suicidology

The goal of the American Association of Suicidology (AAS) is to understand and prevent suicide. AAS promotes research, public awareness programs, education, and training for professionals, survivors, and all interested persons. AAS serves as a national clearinghouse for information on suicide. AAS has many resources and publications, which are available to its membership and the general public. For membership information, please contact:

American Association of Suicidology
5221 Wisconsin Avenue, N. W.
Washington, DC 20015
(202) 237-2280
(202) 237-2282 (Fax)
Email:info@suicidology.org
Website: www.suicidology.org

AMERICAN ASSOCIATION OF SUICIDOLOGY

Dedicated to the Understanding and Prevention of Suicide

Elderly[1] Suicide Fact Sheet

- The elderly made up 12.4% of the population; they accounted for almost 16.7% of all suicides.

- The rate of suicide for the elderly for 2003 was 14.6 per 100,000.

- There was one elderly suicide every 100 minutes. There were about 14 elderly suicides each day, resulting in 5,248 suicides in 2003 among those 65 and older.

- Elderly white men were at the highest risk with a rate of approximately 32 suicides per 100,000 each year.

- White men over the age of 85, who are labeled "old-old", were at the greatest risk of all age-gender-race groups. In 2003, the suicide rate for these men was 51.4 per 100,000. That was 4.8 times the current rate for men of <u>all</u> ages (10.8 per 100,000).

- 85% of elderly suicides were male; the rate of male suicides in late life was 5.5 times greater than for female suicides.

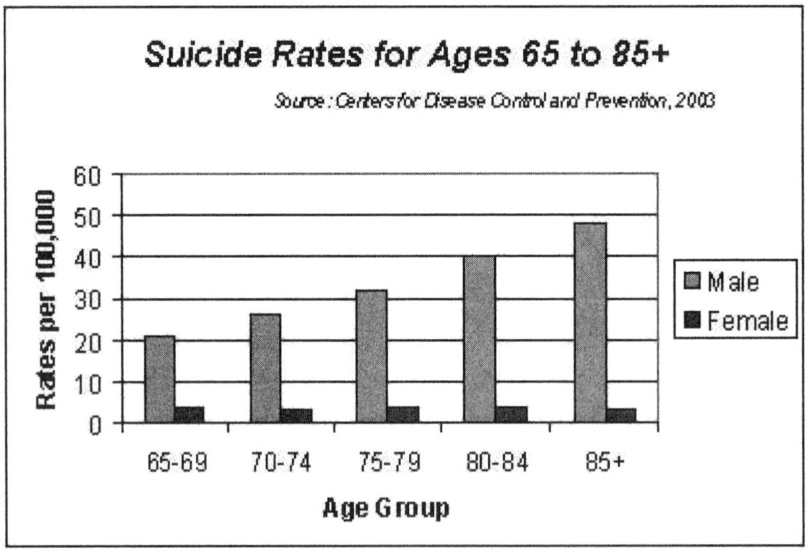

- The rate of suicide for women declined after age 60 (after peaking in middle adulthood, ages 45-49).

[1] In this fact sheet, elderly refers to persons over the age of 65. Unless otherwise specified, information presented refers to the latest available data (i.e., 2003 data).

23 February 2006

- The suicide rate for the elderly reached a peak in 1987 at 21.8 per 100,000 people. Since 1987, the rate of elderly suicides has declined 28% (down to 14.6 in 2003). This is the largest decline in suicide rates among the elderly since the 1930's.

- Although older adults attempt suicide less often than those in other age groups, they have a higher completion rate. For all ages combined, there is an estimated 1 suicide for every 25 attempted suicides. Among the young (15-24 years) there is an estimated 1 suicide for every 100-200 attempts. Over the age of 65, there is one estimated suicide for every 4 attempted suicides.

- In 2003, suicide rates ranged from 12.7 per 100,000 among persons aged 65 to 74, to 16.4 per 100,000 persons aged 75 to 84, to 16.9 per 100,000 persons aged 85 and older.

- Firearms were the most common means (73%) used for completing suicide among the elderly. Men (74%) use firearms more than twice as often as women (34%).

- Alcohol or substance abuse plays a diminishing role in later life suicides compared to younger suicides.

- One of the leading causes of suicide among the elderly is depression, often undiagnosed and/or untreated.

- The act of completing suicide is rarely preceded by only one cause or one reason. In the elderly, common risk factors include:

    - The recent death of a loved one;
    - Physical illness, uncontrollable pain or the fear of a prolonged illness;
    - Perceived poor health;
    - Social isolation and loneliness;
    - Major changes in social roles (e.g. retirement).

Sources

The information for this fact sheet was gathered from the National Center for Injury Prevention and Control (NCIPC) website (http://www.cdc.gov/ncipc/wisqars/default.htm) operated by the Centers for Disease Control and Prevention (CDC).

American Association of Suicidology

The goal of the American Association of Suicidology (AAS) is to understand and prevent suicide. AAS promotes research, public awareness programs, education, and training for professionals, survivors, and all interested persons. AAS serves as a national clearinghouse for information on suicide. AAS has many resources and publications which are available to its membership and the general public. For membership information, please contact:

American Association of Suicidology
5221 Wisconsin Avenue, N.W.
Washington, DC 20015
(202) 237-2280 (202) 237-2282 (Fax)
Email: info@suicidology.org
Website: www.suicidology.org

NOTES

SECTION THREE

Intervention

Intervention

"Asking the question" is sometimes a difficult part of the intervention process. The most effective question is a direct and non-leading question, such as "Have you been thinking of hurting or killing yourself?" This direct phrasing calls for a direct yes or no answer, without biasing the response.

What do you do when someone responds "yes, I am considering suicide?" Risk assessment is the next step. An acronym that captures many of the risk factors in a checklist format is SAD PERSONS. The more factors which are true for the individual, the higher their risk level.

As helpers, we can get caught up in thinking we have to solve all of the suicidal individual's problems in order to keep them alive. It's easy for us to become overwhelmed by their problems. Shneidman's theoretical cubic model helps make the point that we only need to effect a small change to potentially have a large impact.

In Shneidman's model, the three faces of the cube are pain, pressure, and perturbation. Each face of the cube ranges in value from 1 to 5. Thus, the cube with maximum pain, maximum pressure, and maximum perturbation is the 5-5-5 cubelet. When individuals are in this danger zone, they are at high risk for imminent suicide. However, this model also illustrates that if we can help them leave the 5-5-5 cubelet, by even one cubelet in any direction, they are no longer in the imminent danger zone.

We will present the SAFER-R as an effective intervention technique. In this technique, stabilization of the situation is the first step, followed by acknowledging the crisis, facilitating understanding, encouraging effective coping techniques, restoring independent functioning and referring when necessary.

A fear common to many people is that if they mention the word 'suicide' to a mental health professional, they will immediately be hospitalized against their will. The concept of "necessary and sufficient intervention" illustrates that involuntary hospitalization is the last in an escalating series of intervention options. Situation permitting, we use involuntary hospitalization only as a last resort.

Let's start at the beginning and look at asking the question, "Have you been thinking of hurting or killing yourself?"

SAFER-Revised Model

Stabilize the Situation

Acknowledge the Crisis

Facilitate Understanding / Normalize

Encourage Effective Coping Techniques

Recovery or Referral

SAFER-Revised Model
(Everly, 2001)

Stabilization (plus Introduction) [1]

⬇

Acknowledgement [1]
A. Event ⬇ **B. Reactions**

Facilitation of Understanding: Normalization [1]

⬇

Encourage Effective Coping (Mechanisms of Action) [1,2,3]

⬇

Referral? [1, 2, 3]

[1= Assessment, 2= Generate intervention options, 3= Implement interventions]

SAFER-Revised Model

✦ **Stabilize the Situation**
- Mitigate affective escalation.
- Remove from provocative stressors.
- May use a diversion (i.e. walk, coffee, etc.).

✦ **Acknowledge the Crisis**
- What happened?
- Establish rapport and a sense of safety.
- Provide for cathartic ventilation.

✦ **Facilitate Understanding**
- Explain the symptoms.
- Normalize reactions.

SAFER-Revised Model

✦ **Encourage Effective Coping Techniques**
- Teach basic stress survival skills.
- Improve immediate and short term coping.
- Develop a plan for immediate use.

✦ **Recovery or Referral**
- Assess current adaptive functioning.
- Assess need for further assistance.
- If needed, identify appropriate referral.

The Question

Have you been thinking of hurting or killing yourself?

Important Questions

Have you been thinking of hurting or killing yourself?

- ➡When did you last think about suicide?
- ➡How would you kill yourself?
- ➡Do you have the means available?
- ➡Have you ever attempted suicide?
- ➡Has anyone in your family attempted/completed suicide?
- ➡What are the odds that you will kill yourself?
- ➡What has been keeping you alive so far?
- ➡What do you think the future holds in store for you?

Communication Process

Communication Components

Verbal	Vocal
words	tone
content	volume
meaning	inflection

Nonverbal stimuli

facial expression
gesture
body position

Communication Blockades

Personal goals

Rapport

Attitudes, prejudices, frame of reference

Language skills

Environmental distractions

Characteristics of a Good Listener

- Good self image
- Listens intently
- Expresses self clearly
- Honest, empathic
- Focuses on here & now
- Cares about people
- Copes with strong emotion

Common Strong Emotions

Hopelessness

Guilt

Anger

Cognitive Sets

Ambivalence

Tunnel Vision

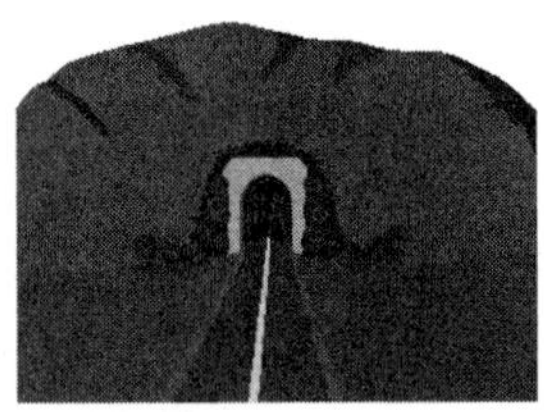

Do's of Intervention

- Remain calm
- Accept their feelings
- Rephrase thoughts
- Focus on central issue
- Stay close
- Emphasize temporary nature of problem
- **Explore resources**

**** Listen ** Listen ** Listen ****

Don'ts of Intervention

Don't overlook signs

- Don't sound shocked
- Don't offer empty promises
- Don't try to cheer him/her up
- Don't debate morality
- Don't assume things will improve
- Don't leave person alone
- Don't keep it a secret

Don't remain the ONLY person helping

Major Predictors of Suicidal Behavior

How:

- ♦ Specificity of their plan
- ♦ Availability of means
- ♦ Lethality of method

History:

- ♦ A prior suicide attempt
- ♦ A family history of suicide behaviors

Help:

- ♦ Resources available

Striking a Balance

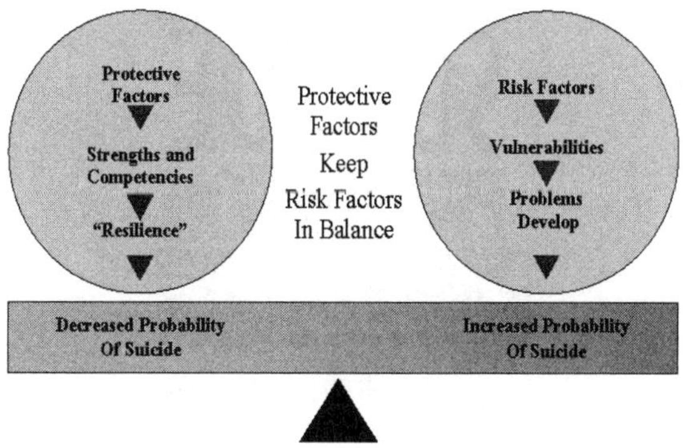

Protective Factors

- Effective coping and problem-solving skills
- Social & family support
- Optimistic outlook
- Sense of "belonging" to a group or organization
- Positive relationships
- Physical activity
- Easily accessible helping resources
- Participation and membership in a community
- Belief that it is okay to ask for help
- Sense of self-efficacy and personal control

AID LIFE

Ask
Intervene immediately
Don't keep it a secret
Locate help
Inform
Find
Expedite

National Hotline

NATIONAL
SUICIDE PREVENTION
LIFELINE™
1-800-273-TALK
www.suicidepreventionlifeline.org
U.S. DEPARTMENT OF HEALTH AND HUMAN SERVICES
Substance Abuse and Mental Health Services Administration
www.samhsa.gov

ACT

www.stopasuicide.org

Acknowledge
- Take it seriously
- Be willing to listen

Care
- Voice your concern
- Reassure – not alone
- Ask about a plan

Treatment
- Referral
- Call 1-800-273-TALK

Problem-solving Approach

Can I change this??

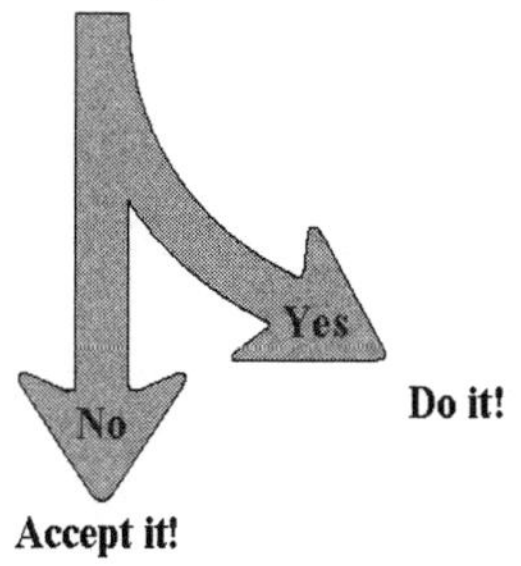

Think Win/Win

	I Lose	I Win
You Win	Lose / Win	Win /Win
You Lose	Lose / Lose	Win / Lose

(from *The Seven Habits of Highly Effective People* by Covey)

Barricades to Seeking Help

Denial

Avoidance

Anger

Fear: seeking help will impact job

Fear: chain of command or supervisor will be contacted

Fear: hospitalization, being stigmatized

Necessary & Sufficient INTERVENTION

(Clark & White, 2003)

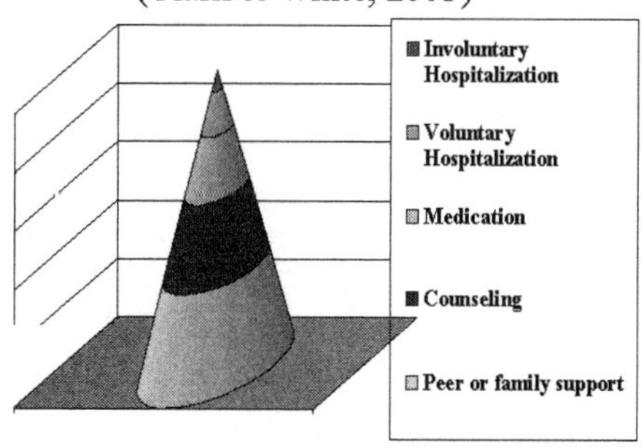

Referral Options

24 hour
- 911
- ER
- Crisis lines
- Hot lines
- EAP
- Peer Support

Professional
- M.D./MHP
- Police
- School Counselor
- Minister/Clergy
- Legal
- Veteran Center
- DSHS
- Psych. Hospital
- Financial

Community
- Family
- Friends
- Red Cross
- Church
- NOVA
- COPS
- S.O.S.
- Mission
- ??A
- United Way
- Salvation Army
- Community Svcs
- Women's Shelter
- Funeral Homes
- Comp. Friends
- Support Groups
- Internet

Observer's Feedback Form #1

Role play – Asking the Question

1. Use of listening skills:

Silence	Body language	Open/closed Q's	Summary
Reflection	Paraphrase	Eye contact	Other:

2. Describe your perception of the role player's rapport:

3. Did the crisis worker ask about suicide openly? Clearly?

4. Did the crisis worker ask about risk factors?

5. Did the intervention follow a structure or appear to have a plan?

   What improvements could be made?

6. Did it appear as if the intervention would be effective?

   What improvements could be made?

GUIDELINES FOR GOOD LISTENING IN CRISIS SITUATIONS

Diane Myers, R.N., M.S.N.

- ***PREPARE TO LISTEN:*** Make sure you have the time and place to truly listen. If time is limited, acknowledge the fact and make the most of the time you have. If necessary, arrange another time to talk. If possible, choose a quiet place. Cut down distractions and interruptions.

- ***SHOW INTEREST:*** Face the person. Keep a relaxed posture. Encourage communication with gestures (like a nod of the head), phrases ("I see," "go on"), or facial expression.

- ***BE AWARE OF CULTURAL PREFERENCES:*** Different cultures have different customs regarding nonverbal contact (leaning forward, eye contact), distances for interaction, and touch.

- ***RESPECT THE INDIVIDUAL'S SITUATION:*** Do not probe for feelings when a person is numb or in shock. Do not try to talk a person out of their feelings or anger. Respect the times when a person may not want to talk about how things are going. If in doubt, ask the person what they would like at the moment.

- ***BE AWARE OF NONVERBAL COMMUNICATION:*** Fidgeting hands may indicate nervousness, while a clenched fist or jaw may indicate anger and a tapping foot may indicate impatience. If a person steps back from you or stiffens in posture or looks away, it may indicate that you have invaded their personal space and they are more comfortable with a little distance. Crossed arms may indicate defensiveness. Pay attention to eye contact, tone of voice, posture, and emotional tone.

- ***PROVIDE COMFORT:*** Help to make the person physically comfortable: offer a chair, food, a beverage, a blanket, or whatever else might seem helpful. Touch may be comforting but be sensitive to the person's reaction, especially if the person is a victim of assault.

- ***FOCUS ATTENTION:*** Center on the person and their situation. Try to give your undivided attention, although this can be difficult if the situation is chaotic. Be alert, present, and receptive.

- ***LISTEN CAREFULLY:*** Listen to words, nonverbal communication, and feelings. Try to listen without judging, moralizing, condemning, making assumptions, or drawing conclusions. Do not lose track of what the person is saying because you are caught up in planning a response.

- ***AVOID INTERRUPTING:*** If time and circumstances allow, let the person to finish speaking before responding. Try not to jump in at every pause, finish statements for the person, or hurry them along.

- ***RESPECT SILENCES:*** Silences can be very important. They can allow the person time and space to think something through, or to allow a feeling to surface.

- ***ALLOW EXPRESSIONS OF EMOTION:*** Do not try to prevent expressions of emotion, such as crying, by interrupting. The expression of feeling can be therapeutic, and it is likely that the person will be better able to continue after intense emotions have been released. A touch or nod of the head can indicate that you empathize.

- ***TOLERATE REPETITION:*** Often, a person in crisis needs to tell the same story, or to go over certain information many times. It is an important part of "working through" the trauma and "making sense" of what has happened. In addition, the person may need for you to repeat what you have said to them, or to repeat specific instructions or questions. A person in crisis often feels overwhelmed, and memory lapses and confusion are normal.

- ***ASK SIMPLE, CLEAR QUESTIONS:*** Ask questions one at a time. Keep them understandable and focused. Use closed-ended questions (that can be answered with a "yes" or "no") only to establish facts. Open-ended questions (such as "how" or "what") bring out more information. Questions can be specific ("What happened to your apartment in the September 11 attacks?) or more general ("Tell me how it's been for you and your family since September 11?) Always wait for a response to each question you ask.

- ***BE SURE YOU UNDERSTAND:*** Periodically check to be sure you clearly understand what the person is telling you. By doing so, you will also be validating the person's remarks, demonstrating your attentiveness, and confirming your interest. The following methods can be helpful:

    - ***Restating or reflexive questioning:*** Repeating a term or phrase the person has said for the purpose of inquiring about it or emphasizing it. Example: "I feel I'm acting like a real jerk." "A real jerk?" Don't overdo this method or you will sound like a parrot.

    - ***Paraphrasing:*** Making a statement that puts into your own words what you think you have heard. Example: "I look at my kids and wonder what they're thinking." "You're really concerned about how your children are taking all of this."

    - ***Reflection of feelings:*** Expressing the stated or implied feelings you have heard. Example: "I feel like no one can understand what I'm going through." "That sounds very lonely."

    - ***Asking for clarification:*** Simple questioning when the person's meaning is unclear. Example: "I'm concerned about my wife." "What is it that concerns you?"

    - ***Summarizing:*** Reviewing major points that have been covered in order to ensure you have heart what's most important.

- ***WAIT-THINK-RESPOND:*** Waiting helps you to think, and thinking increases the chance that your response will be appropriate. A short pause is usually all that is needed.

- ***SHARE YOURSELF:*** Thoughtfully sharing a little bit of yourself or your emotions can let the person know that you empathize. A tear in your eye is fine; torrents of tears are not. It may comfort the person to know that you once went through a similar crisis. However, be careful not to be take over the conversation by sharing a lengthy story of your own trauma. The person will then feel they need to take care of you. Be careful about giving advice; what you would do in the situation may not be right for this person. Try instead to help the person problem-solve.

➢ ***GIVE HOPE:*** Without giving false reassurance, contradicting the person's feelings, or providing your personal religious beliefs, provide any positive information or thoughts you have about the situation. For example, "The earthquake damage to your apartment was substantial, but I'm glad you have found that most of your furnishings and belongings are in good shape." Without being condescending, point out positive steps the individual has made, even if they are small. In a crisis, individuals often lose perspective and do not appreciate the positive steps they are making.

➢ ***"BE" WITH THE PERSON, EVEN IF YOU CAN'T "FIX IT":*** Simply being present, listening, and empathizing can be incredibly helpful and strengthening to the person in crisis. Don't underestimate your value as a good listener.

References

American Red Cross (1982). *Providing Red Cross disaster health services.* ARC 3076.

Hafen, B.Q. & Frandsen, K.J. (1985). *Psychological emergencies and crisis intervention.* Englewood, CO: Morton Publishing Company.

Mitchell, J.T. & Bray, G. (1990). *Emergency services stress: Guidelines for preserving the health and careers of emergency services personnel.* Englewood Cliffs, NJ: Prentice Hall, Inc.

Mitchell, J.T. & Resnick, H.L.P. (1981). *Emergency response to crisis.* Bowie, MD: Robert J. Brady, Co.

Zunin, L.M. & Zunin, H.S. (1991). *The art of condolence: What to write, what to say, what to do at a time of loss.* New York: Harper Collins Publishers.

Diane Myers, R.N., M.S.N., 1992; 2002.

AMERICAN ASSOCIATION OF SUICIDOLOGY

Dedicated to the Understanding and Prevention of Suicide

IF YOU ARE CONSIDERING SUICIDE

The last thing that most people expect is that they will run out of reasons to live. But if you are experiencing suicidal thoughts, you need to know that you're not alone. By some estimates, as many as one in six people will become seriously suicidal at some point in their lives. Fortunately, most people do not act on their suicidal thoughts – crises pass and problems are solved. But sometimes thoughts lead to self-harm.

Some Important Facts AAS Would Like to Share with You

Suicidal thinking is usually associated with problems that can be treated. Clinical depression, anxiety disorders, chemical dependency, and other disorders produce profound emotional distress. They also interfere with effective problem-solving. But you need to know that new treatments are available, and studies show that the vast majority of people who receive appropriate treatment improve or recover completely. Even if you have received treatment before, you should know that different treatments work better for different people in different situations. Several tries are sometimes necessary before the right combination is found.

If you are unable to think of solutions other than suicide, it is not that solutions don't exist, only that you are currently unable to see them. Therapists and counselors (and sometimes friends) can help you to see solutions that otherwise are not apparent to you.

Suicidal crises are almost always temporary. Although it might seem as if your unhappiness will never end, it is important to realize that crises are usually time-limited. Solutions are found, feelings change, unexpected positive events occur. Suicide is sometimes referred to as "a permanent solution to a temporary problem." Don't let suicide rob you of better times that would have come you way, if only more time had been allowed to pass

Problems are seldom as great as they appear at first glance. Job loss, financial problems, loss of important people in our lives – all such stressful events can seem catastrophic at the time they are happening. Then, month or years later, they usually look smaller and more manageable. Sometimes, imagining ourselves "five years down the road" can help us to see that a problem that currently seems catastrophic will pass and that we will survive.

Reasons for living can help sustain a person in pain. A famous psychologist once conducted a study of Nazi concentration camp survivors, and found that those who survived almost always reported strong beliefs about what was important in life. You, too, might be able to strengthen your connection with life if you consider what has sustained you through hard times in the past. Family ties, religion, love of art or nature, and dreams for the future are just a few of the many aspects of life that provide meaning and gratification, but which we can lose sight of due to emotional distress.

Do not keep suicidal thoughts to yourself! Help is available for you, whether through a friend, therapist, or member of the clergy. Find someone you trust and let them know how bad things are. This can be your first step on the road to healing.

Telephone Numbers for More Information on Receiving Help

National Mental Health Association	703-684-7722
Anxiety Disorders Association of America	301-231-9350
American Psychological Association	202-336-5500
American Psychiatric Association	202-682-6000
Depressive and Manic-Depressive Association	312-642-0049
National Alliance for the Mentally Ill	703-524-7600
National Suicide Prevention Lifeline	800-273-TALK (800-273-8255)

Other web sites to visit:

The Samaritans (http://www.samaritans.org.uk/)
Psych Central (http://www.grohol.com/helpme.htm)
Metanoia (http://www.metanoia.org/suicide/)
Befrienders International (http://www.befrienders.org)

American Association of Suicidology

The goal of the American Association of Suicidology (AAS) is to understand and prevent suicide. AAS promotes research, public awareness programs, education, and training for professionals, survivors, and all interested persons. AAS serves as a national clearinghouse for information on suicide. AAS has many resources and publications that are available to its membership and the general public. For membership information, please contact:

American Association of Suicidology
5221 Wisconsin Avenue, N. W.
Washington, DC 20015
Phone: (202) 237-2280
Fax (202) 237-2282
Website: www.suicidology.org
Email: info@suicidology.org

Understanding and Helping the Suicidal Individual

BE AWARE OF THE WARNING SIGNS

Are you or someone you love at risk of suicide? Get the facts and take appropriate action.

Get help immediately by contacting a mental health professional or calling 1-800-273-8255 for a referral should you witness, hear, or see anyone exhibiting any one or more of the following:

- Someone threatening to hurt or kill him/herself, or taking of wanting to hurt or kill him/herself.
- Someone looking for ways to kill him/herself by seeking access to firearms, available pills, or other means.
- Someone talking or writing about death, dying or suicide, when these actions are out of the ordinary for the person.

Seek help as soon as possible by contacting a mental health professional or calling 1-800-273-8255 for a referral should you witness, hear, or see anyone exhibiting any one or more of the following:

- Hopelessness
- Rage, uncontrolled anger, seeking revenge
- Acting reckless or engaging in risky activities, seemingly without thinking
- Feeling trapped – like there's no way out
- Increased alcohol or drug use
- Withdrawing from friends, family and society
- Anxiety, agitation, unable to sleep or sleeping all the time
- Dramatic mood changes
- No reason for living; no sense of purpose in life

BE AWARE OF THE FACTS

1. Suicide is preventable. Most suicidal individuals desperately want to live; they are just unable to see alternatives to their problems.
2. Most suicidal individuals give definite warnings of their suicidal intentions, but others are either unaware of the significance of these warnings or do not know how to respond to them.
3. Talking about suicide does not cause someone to be suicidal.
4. Approximately 32,000 Americans kill themselves every year. The number of suicide attempts is much greater and often results in serious injury.
5. Suicide is the third leading cause of death among young people ages 15-24, and it is the eighth leading cause of death among all persons.
6. Youth (15-24) suicide rates increased more than 200% from the 1950's to the late 1970's. Following the late 1970's, the rates for youth suicide have remained stable.

7. The suicide rate is higher among the elderly (over 65) than any other age group.
8. Four times as many men kill themselves as compared to women, yet three times as many women attempt suicide as compared to men.
9. Suicide cuts across all age, economic, social, and ethnic boundaries.
10. Firearms are currently the most utilized method of suicide by essentially all groups (male, female, young, old, white, non-white).
11. Surviving family members not only suffer the trauma of losing a loved one to suicide, and may themselves be at higher risk for suicide and emotional problems.

WAYS TO BE HELPFUL TO SOMEONE WHO IS THREATENING SUICIDE

1. Be aware. Learn the warning signs.
2. Get involved. Become available. Show interest and support.
3. Ask if he/she is thinking about suicide.
4. Be direct. Talk openly and freely about suicide.
5. Be willing to listen. Allow for expression of feelings. Accept the feelings.
6. Be non-judgmental. Don't debate whether suicide is right or wrong, or feelings are good or bad. Don't lecture on the value of life.
7. Don't dare him/her to do it.
8. Don't give advice by making decisions for someone else to tell them to behave differently.
9. Don't ask 'why'. This encourages defensiveness.
10. Offer empathy, not sympathy.
11. Don't act shocked. This creates distance.
12. Don't be sworn to secrecy. Seek support.
13. Offer hope that alternatives are available, do not offer glib reassurance; it only proves you don't understand.
14. Take action! Remove means! Get help from individuals or agencies specializing in crisis intervention and suicide prevention.

BE AWARE OF FEELINGS, THOUGHTS, AND BEHAVIORS

Nearly everyone at some time in his or her life thinks about suicide. Most everyone decides to live because they come to realize that the crisis is temporary, but death is not. On the other hand, people in the midst of a crisis often perceive their dilemma as inescapable and feel an utter loss of control. Frequently, they:

- Can't stop the pain
- Can't think clearly
- Can't make decisions
- Can't see any way out
- Can't sleep, eat or work
- Can't get out of the depression
- Can't make the sadness of away
- Can't see the possibility of change
- Can't see themselves as worthwhile
- Can't get someone's attention
- Can't see to get control

TALK TO SOMEONE – YOU ARE NOT ALONE

CONTACT:

- A community mental health agency
- A school counselor or psychologist
- A suicide prevention/crisis intervention center
- A private therapist
- A family physician
- A religious/spiritual leader

American Association of Suicidology
5521 Wisconsin Avenue, NW
Washington, DC 20015
Phone: (202) 237-2280
Fax: (202) 237-2280
Email: info@suicidology.org
Website: www.suicidology.org

NOTES

SECTION FOUR

Postvention

Suicide Postvention

Postvention, (Shneidman, 1981) in contrast to prevention, describes the actions and services provided to survivors of suicide. These **suicide survivors** include spouses, significant others, parents, children, grandparents, aunts, uncles, cousins, lovers, friends, co-workers, classmates, etc. Anyone of us may be touched by the suicide of someone we care about.

Suicide survivors struggle with a myriad of emotions, from grief and loss through anger and guilt. Their grief is often complicated but not pathological. The suicide may be sudden and unexpected or a process which may have seemed inevitable to family and friends. The suicide often leaves "unfinished business" with which the survivors struggle for months and possibly years.

They proceed through a gamut of emotions. Similar to anyone struggling with a loss, the initial reactions may be shock, numbness, and denial of the death. Added to that is the denial of the death as a suicide. This denial may be related to religious concerns or even concerns about their own susceptibility to suicide.

Survivors often engage in a prolonged search for "why?" Why did my loved one/friend leave me? Why didn't I prevent their suicide? Why did they do this to me (Jordan, 2001)?

There is no doubt that family members are deeply affected by losing a loved one to suicide. Researchers and professionals who work with organizations are recognizing that coworkers, and even the organization itself, can be deeply affected by a suicide of an employee. Recent emphasis has been given to providing postvention services to law enforcement, EMS, military personnel, and students and teachers who have experienced a suicide within their organization.

Postvention is currently seen as a natural extension to suicide prevention and intervention programs. Postvention policies and procedures are a necessary component to any suicide prevention program because there will always be a base level of suicide no matter how effective a suicide prevention program may be. Suicide survivors can be viewed as victims with post-traumatic stress and as such are in need of assistance in dealing with thoughts and reactions, both immediately following the event and as they begin their grief experience (Loo, 2001).

An effective postvention program includes written policies and procedures that are supported by an organization's leadership prior to an event. Postvention services should provide practical advice to coworkers in dealing with family members of the deceased. These programs should also assist coworkers and management in dealing with the loss of an employee, plus provide referral resources to individuals who are struggling excessively with anger, loss or guilt.

Postvention education provides management with an understanding that normal group performance and work productivity may be disrupted for quite a while. It can help senior leaders to sensitively and effectively deal with the effects that the suicide may have on their organization.

Definition of Suicide Survivor

Family members and others who survive following the death of their loved one by suicide

Suicide survivors include spouses, significant others, parents, children, grandparents, aunts, uncles, cousins, lovers, friends, co-workers, classmates, etc.

Survivor Reactions

High risk groups

"Stigma spillover" → Parents, Spouses/Significant Others

Parents

Spouses/Significant Others

Children/Siblings

Those who find the body

Those who witness the suicide

Grief reactions

Similar but different...

- Similar to loss due to any sudden or violent death
- Often compromises usual mourning rituals
- Expect a 4-7 year recovery period
- Typically not pathological but often complicated
  - Death is usually sudden and unexpected
  - Leaves "unfinished business" - no closure
  - Rejection, abandonment
  - Often leaves a violent death scene
  - Scene is a "crime scene"
  - Media involvement

Bereavement Issues

Knieper (SLTB, 29(4), 353-364)

Normal (Kubler-Ross, 1969)

- ✓ Denial
- ✓ Anger
- ✓ Bargaining
- ✓ Depression
- ✓ Acceptance

Complicated

- ✓ Guilt
- ✓ Embarrassment
- ✓ Rejection
- ✓ Shame
- ✓ Isolation
- ✓ Search for meaning

Survivor Reactions
"Survivor Syndrome"

Shock

Numbness

Denial of death

Denial of death as a Suicide

Religious concerns

Prolonged search for "Why??"

Fear of personal susceptibility

Survivor Reactions
Emotional

Shame
Guilt (should'a, could'a, would'a)
Responsibility
Blaming
Scapegoating
Abandonment

****Anger****

Survivor Reactions
Interpersonal

Loneliness
Social Isolation*
Social stigma
Diminished social supports
Difficulty trusting others
Negative family relations
Over protectiveness
Changes in lifestyle (2[d] losses) *

Helping Survivors

Survivor's

don't

get over it *

Helping Survivors
Let them talk

Use deceased's name

Begin ASAP

Repetition = part of healing

Be active listener

Listen without judgement

Encourage positive and negative memories

Helping Survivors
Let them talk

Listen for themes (Jordan, 2001)

➨Why did they do it?

➨Why didn't I prevent it?

➨Why did they do this to me?

In children:

➔Why didn't they love me enough to stay?

➔What did I do that was so bad?

Helping Survivors
Let them talk

Helpful phrases

- ✪ I'm sorry for your loss…
- ✪ How can I help?
- ✪ Is there anyone I can call for you?
- ✪ Since the suicide, what are the biggest challenges for you?
- ✪ When your friend/loved one died, what else died?
- ✪ What one small thing can you do differently that might help you?

Phrases to avoid

- ☹ You know they went to hell…
- ☹ You are young enough to have another child.
- ☹ You have to snap out of it.
- ☹ Get over it.
- ☹ Didn't you see this coming?
- ☹ What did you do to make him/her do this?
- ☹ Crying won't bring him/her back to life.
- ☹ Try to think positive…
- ☹ I know how you feel.

Helping Survivors
Recommendations for Parents

Don't take on new work responsibilities

Talk with other bereaved parents

Talk with significant other

Accept that genders grieve differently

Don't remind parents of their other "blessings"

Watch other children

Helping Survivors

Ask how they are doing

Read about grief, loss, suicide

Take one day at a time

Remind them of positive memories

Invite them for a visit

Communicate with compassion

"I'll listen when you want to talk"

"Hindering" Survivors

Denying the death as a suicide

Ignoring or not taking the problem seriously

Pressuring them to "get over it"

Self-medicating/Taking them drinking

Offering negative religious judgments

Being judgmental

Using reverse psychology - "Do it"

Keeping it secret

Trying to convince them they are not suicidal

Helping Survivors

After time

Support/self-help groups

Memorials

Facilitate a grieving ritual

Be aware of special days

Helping others helps themselves

Faith/spiritual beliefs

Survivor conferences

Don't hurry grief!!

Postvention is Prevention!

"Effective postvention for suicidally bereaved families may be one of the most important forms of multigenerational prevention available to mental health professionals."

Jordan, J.R. (2001). ***Is Suicide Bereavement Different? A Reassessment of the Literature.*** **Suicide and Life Threatening Behavior, 31(1), 99.**

Organizational Implications
CISM rationale

- Highly disruptive to both individuals & organization
- Leaves a long term, complicated impact on co-workers and peers
- Triggers a range of emotions - shock, confusion, frustration, anger, grief, guilt, depression, insecurity, etc.
- May disrupt normal group performance for an extended time, polarization may occur
- Need management/union support

Consulting with Media

When reporting on a suicide, include:

- prevention efforts
- therapy and crisis options
- importance of openly discussing suicide
- describe deceased as "having died by suicide" *(or method)* rather than as "a suicide"

www.afsp.org

Consulting with Media

When reporting on a suicide, avoid:

- romanticizing the act
- detailed descriptions/photos of method
- presenting suicide as an inexplicable act of an otherwise healthy individual
- referring to completed suicides as "successful"

www.afsp.org

CISM Applications

- Pre-incident education, preparation
- Assessment
- Strategic Planning
- Large Group Crisis Intervention:
  - Demobilizations, Respite/Rehab Sectors, CMB
- Small Group Crisis Intervention:
  - Defusings, CMB
  - "Debriefing" Models : CISD; HERD; NOVA; Multi-stressor debriefing model; CED
- One-on-one crisis intervention
- Family CISM
- Organizational/Community intervention/consultation
- Pastoral crisis intervention
- Follow-up and referral for continued care

Strategic Planning Formula: The five T's approach

- Target – Who needs assistance who does not?
- Type – What type of assistance do they need?
- Timing – When will that assistance be most useful and when will circumstances allow it?
- Theme – What themes, issues, concerns should be considered to build the right intervention package? What has happened? What will happen?
- Teams (Resources) – What resources will it take to provide the right interventions at the right time?

A further note on "Theme"

- "Theme" refer to any circumstance, issue or concern that influences strategic decision making
- "Theme" also refers to any circumstance, issue or concern that influences the choice of specific crisis intervention tactics

RELATIVE INTENSITY OF GROUP INTERVENTIONS

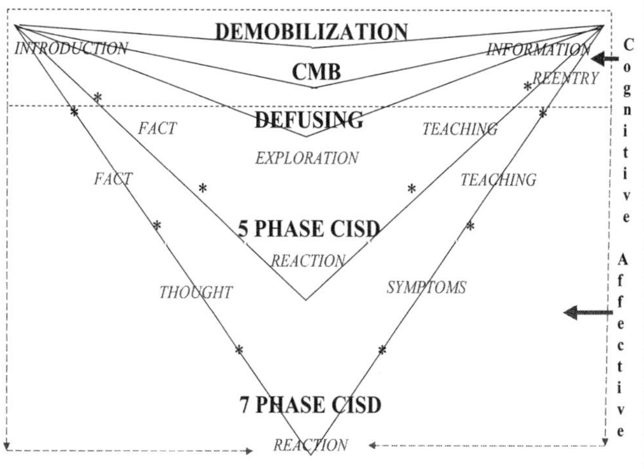

Organizational Implications

CISM applications

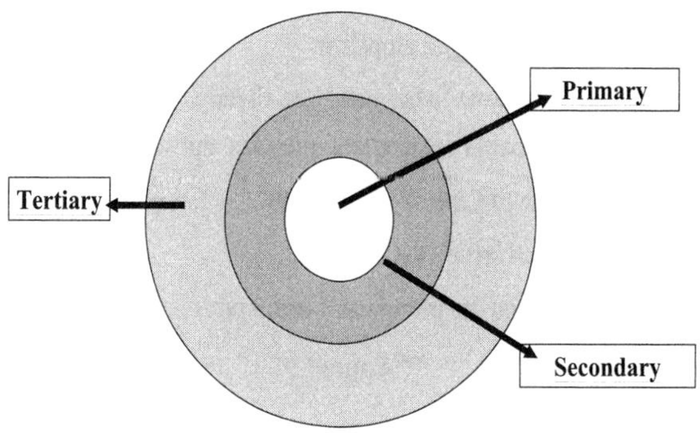

Organizational Implications
CISM applications

Target	Type	Timing	Theme	Resources

Organizational Implications
What to expect in a CISD

- Why, why, why...
- But, but, but…
- S/he was so happy
- My religion says…
- Should have...
- Could have...
- Would have...

- Anger
- Frustration
- Grief, guilt
- Loss
- Feel out of control
- Depression
- Vulnerability
- Feel empty

Organizational Implications
CISM issues

- Offer understanding & empathy
- Don't try to answer 'why' question directly. Better to say, "we wish we could answer that question, but we cannot."
- Do not equate to Line of Duty Death
- Deal with each issue as it arises
- Suggest feelings the group can't bring up

****Anger****

Organizational Implications
CISM issues (cont.)

- Provide practical advice on dealing with family members of the deceased
- Provide practical advice to organization
- Help the group care about the person, and accept the choice he or she made
- Refer individuals who are struggling excessively with anger, loss, or guilt

LODD vs. Suicide

LODD	Suicide
Continued support	Cut off from support
Praised for work	Achievements minimized
Public outpouring of support	Private shame and guilt
National Police week	Nothing
Extensive support network	Support network collapses
Increased benefits	Decreased benefits

Organizational Implications

CISM issues

Always remember to Care for the Caregivers

Helping the Helpers

Both personal and professional issues

Personal issues similar to suicide survivor issues

Psychologists – 22% and Psychiatrists - 50% chance of a completed patient suicide (Ramsay and Newman, 2005)

Helping the Helpers

Personal issues

Affective

Anger
Sadness/Depression
Relief

May lead to…

Blame
Fuels guilt, denial, anger
**Guilt

Cognitive

Denial/Repression
Guilt
Shame

Myth-making
Obsessive reviewing
Fuels professional fear

Don't hurry grief!!

Helping the Helpers

Professional issues

Adequacy/competency	**May lead to…**
Sense of personal failure	Conservatism
Shattered self-confidence	Decrease in emergency tx
	Professional shift
Fears	
Blame by family	Avoid family, funeral
Censure by peers	Secrecy, isolation
Damage to reputation	Leaving profession
Reorganization	Formal case review
What can I learn??	Enhanced competency

Keeping Patients Alive

Put weight on the side of **Life**

Help them help themselves

Only they can 'unstick' themselves

Deceased bears the ultimate responsibility

Summary

Awareness

Prevention

Intervention

Postvention

Summary of Commonly Used Crisis Intervention Tactics

INTERVENTION	TIMING	TARGET GROUP	POTENTIAL GOALS
Pre-event Planning/ Preparation	Pre-event	Anticipated target / victim population	Anticipatory guidance, foster resistance, resilience.
Assessment	Pre-intervention	Those directly & indirectly exposed	Determiniation of need for intervention.
Strategic planning	Pre-event and during event	Anticipated exposed and victim populations	Improve overall crisis response.
Individual Crisis Intervention (including "psychological first aid")	As needed	Individuals as needed	Assessment, screening, education, normalization, reduction of acute distress, triage, and facilitation of continued support.
Large Group Crisis Intervention			
* Demobilization	Shift disengagement, end of deployment	Emergency personnel	Decompression, ease transition, screening, triage education and meet basic needs.
* Respite center	Ongoing, large scale events	Emergency personnel, large groups	Respite, refreshment, screening, triage and support.
* Crisis Management Briefing (CMB) and large group "psychological first aid"	As needed	Heterogeneous large groups	Inform, control rumors, increase cohesion.
Small Group Crisis Intervention			
* Small Group Crisis Management Briefing (sCMB).	On-going and post-event; may be repeated as needed	Small groups seeking infomation / resources	Information, control rumors, reduce acute distress, increase cohesion, facilitate resilience, screening and triage.

Summary of Commonly Used Crisis Intervention Tactics

INTERVENTION	TIMING	TARGET GROUP	POTENTIAL GOALS
Small Group Crisis Intervention (continued)			
* Defusing (and small group "psychological first aid")	On-going events and post-events (≤ 12 hours)	Small homogeneous groups	Stabilization, ventilation, reduce acute distress, screening, information, increase cohesion, and facilitate resilience
* Group debriefing (CISD, PD, NOVA MSD, CED, HERD)	Post - event; ~ 1 - 10 days for acute incidents, ~ 3 - 4 weeks post - disaster recovery phase	Small homogeneous groups with equal trauma exposure (e.g., workgroups, emergency services, military)	Increase cohesion, ventilation, information, normalization, reduce acute distress, facilitate resilience, screening and triage. Follow-up essential.
Family Crisis Intervention	Pre-event; as needed	Families	Wide range of interventions (e.g., pre-event preparation, individual crisis intervention, sCMB, CISD or other group processes.)
Organizational / Community Intervention, Consultation	Pre-event; as needed	Organizations affected by trauma or disaster	Improve organizational preparedness and response. Leadership consultation.
Pastoral Crisis Intervention	As needed	Individuals, small groups, large groups, congregations, and communities who desire faith - based presence / crisis intervention	Faith - based support
Follow - up referral	As needed	Intervention recipients and exposed indivduals	Assure continuity of care

SUMMARY
CRITICAL INCIDENT STRESS MANAGEMENT
GROUP PROCEDURES

TYPE	DEMOBILIZATION	CRISIS MANAGEMENT BRIEFING	DEFUSING	DEBRIEFING CISD
WHEN	After Shift	Anytime post-crisis	Within 12 hours	24 hours – 10 days*
WHO	Large # of responders	Organizations / Schools Communities	Small groups	Small groups
FORMAT	Information & Rest	Information & Resources	3 Stages	7 Stages
LEADER	Peer, chaplain, mental health	Peer, chaplain and / or mental health	Peer, chaplain or mental health	At least one mental health trained leader
LENGTH	½ hour	1 – 1½ hours	20 – 45 minutes	1 ½ - 3 hours
FOLLOW - UP **	CISD	Assess need for CISD	Assess need for CISD	Closure or referral

* Debriefings for disasters may not be appropriate until 2 – 4 weeks (and sometimes longer) following the disaster.

** During and following all group processes the need for 1 : 1 follow-up is always assessed.

Joyce LiBethe, PhD

School Postvention Scenario

After lunch a group of Sunnyville High School students are practicing for the play "Romeo and Juliet". There are approximately 35 students, and the High School Art, English, Drama, Band and Choir instructors in the school auditorium. Suddenly while everyone seems to be taking their places, amid much talking and laughing, a sound is heard above the noise. Students and teachers are saying "what was that" "It sounded like a shot, no two shots." Immediately students begin to panic. The Drama instructor runs to the back of the stage where the shots seemed to come from and finds two students in a pool of blood. The instructor quickly calls out for someone to call 911. She checks for a pulse but cannot find one for either of the students. Students are rushing up to see what has happened and before the instructor can keep them back, they see their classmates lying on the stage surrounded by blood. Several students scream and then start crying. The other instructors make their way through the students trying to get them back from the scene and they too are confronted with the deathly scene of the two students. The English instructor states that Mike and Christie have talked about running away and being together, but she had no idea that they would do something like this. Allan, a friend of Mike's said that Christie's parents didn't want her dating Mike, she needed to concentrate on graduating from high school and go to college.

A student ran to the front office and notified the secretary to call 911. The principal and school nurse returned with him and viewed the scene. The principal asked the instructors to take the students to a classroom off of the auditorium and supply him the names of all of the students who were present at the time this happened. Sirens are heard and shortly after the police and EMS arrive. The EMS personnel are shocked to find out it is the Chief's son who is dead.

The principal notifies the secretary over the intercom to contact the county CISM director and have her report immediately.

Task:

You are the CISM director, and responsible for providing services to all county, city, public employees within the county. You have approximately 30 trained CISM team members from various local agencies. You are also able to access assistance through the State mutual aid which can contact teams throughout the state, including school CISM teams. What would you recommend to the high school principal regarding CISM interventions to this incident?

Identify groups to receive services.

How many CISM team members will be needed?

Where will the interventions be held?

Are there any special considerations or especially difficult situations that need to be dealt with?

CISM Applications Matrix

Target	Type	Timing	Theme	Resources

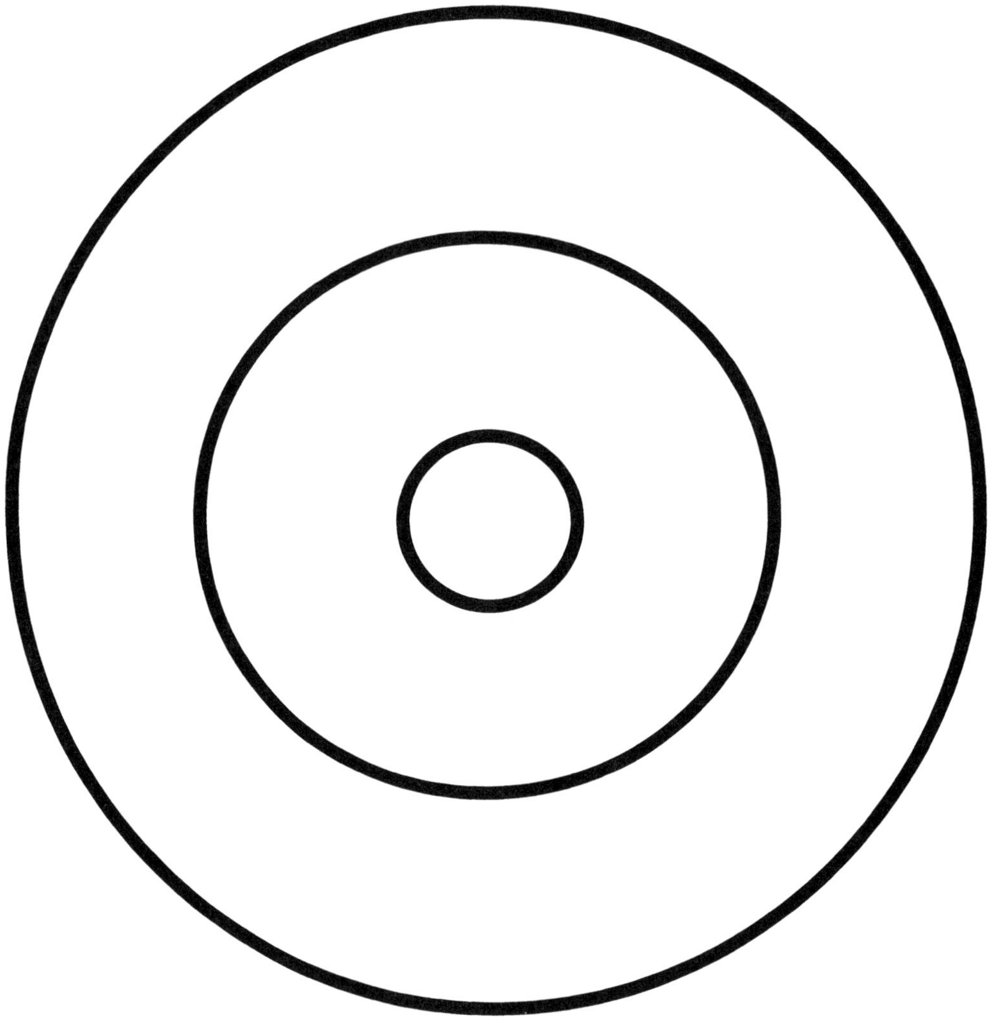

Inner circle: Primary group

Middle circle: Secondary group

Outer circle: Tertiary group

Beyond Surviving: Suggestions for Survivors

Iris M. Bolton

1. Know you can survive; you may not think so, but you can.
2. Struggle with "why" it happened until you no longer need to know "why" or until YOU are satisfied with partial answers.
3. Know you may feel overwhelmed by the intensity of your feelings but that all your feelings are normal.
4. Anger, guilt, confusion, forgetfulness are common responses. You are not crazy, you are in mourning.
5. Be aware you may feel appropriate anger at the person, at the world, at God, at yourself. It's okay to express it.
6. You may feel guilty for what you think you did or did not do. Guilt can turn into regret, through forgiveness.
7. Having suicidal thoughts is common. It does not mean that you will act on those thoughts.
8. Remember to take one moment or one day at a time.
9. Find a good listener with whom to share. Call someone if you need to talk.
10. Don't be afraid to cry. Tears are healing.
11. Give yourself time to heal.
12. Remember, the choice was not yours. No one is the sole influence on another's life.
13. Expect setbacks. If emotions return like a tidal wave, you may only be experiencing a remnant of grief, an unfinished piece.
14. Try to put off major decisions.
15. Give yourself permission to get professional help.
16. Be aware of the pain in your family and friends.
17. Be patient with yourself and others who may not understand.
18. Set your own limits and learn to say no.
19. Steer clear of people who want to tell you what or how to feel.
20. Know that there are support groups that can be helpful, such as Compassionate Friends or Survivors of Suicide groups. If not, ask a professional to start one.
21. Call on your personal faith to help you through.
22. It is common to experience physical reaction to your grief, e.g. headaches, loss of appetite, inability to sleep.
23. The willingness to laugh with other and at yourself is healing.
24. Wear out your questions, anger, guilt, or other feelings until you can let them go. Letting go doesn't mean forgetting.
25. Know that you will never be the same again, but you can survive and even go beyond just surviving.

AMERICAN ASSOCIATION OF SUICIDOLOGY

Dedicated to the Understanding and Prevention of Suicide

Survivors of Suicide Fact Sheet

A survivor of suicide is a family member or friend of a person who died by suicide.

Some Facts...

Survivors of suicide represent "the largest mental health casualties related to suicide" (Edwin Shneidman, Ph.D., AAS Founding President).

There are currently almost 31,000 suicides annually in the USA. It is estimated that for every suicide there are at least 6 survivors. Some suicidologists believe this to be a very conservative estimate.

Based on this estimate, approximately 5 million American became survivors of suicide in the last 25 years.

About Suicidal Grief

The loss of a loved one by suicide is often shocking, painful and unexpected. The grief that ensues can be intense, complex, and long term. Grief work is an extremely individual and unique process; each person will experience it in their own way and at their own pace.

Grief does not follow a linear path. Furthermore, grief doesn't always move in a forward direction.

There is no time frame for grief. Survivors should not expect that their lives will return to their prior state. Survivors aim to adjust to life without their loved one.

Common emotions experienced in grief are:

Shock	Denial	Pain
Guilt	Anger	Shame
Dispair	Disbelief	Hopelessness
Stress	Sadness	Numbness
Rejection	Loneliness	Abandonment
Confusion	Self-blame	Anxiety
Helplessness	Depression	

These feelings are normal reactions and the expression of them is a natural part or grieving. At first, and periodically during the following days/months of grieving, survivors may feel overwhelmed by their emotions. It is important to take things one day at a time.

Crying is the expression of sadness; it is therefore a natural reaction after the loss of a loved one.

June 20, 2006

Survivors often struggle with the reasons why the suicide occurred and whether they could have done something to prevent the suicide or help their loved one. Feelings of guilt typically ensue if the survivor believes their loved one's suicide could have been prevented.

At times, especially if the loved one had a mental disorder, the survivor may experience relief.

There is a stigma attached to suicide, partly due to the misunderstanding surrounding it. As such, family members and friends of the survivor may not know what to say or how and when to provide assistance. They may rely on the survivor's initiative to talk about the loved one or to ask for help.

Shame or embarrassment might prevent the survivor from reaching out for help. Stigma, ignorance and uncertainty might prevent others from giving the necessary support and understanding. Ongoing support remains important to maintain family and friendship relations during the grieving process.

Survivors sometimes feel that others are blaming them for the suicide. Survivors may feel the need to deny what happened or hide their feelings. This will most likely exacerbate and complicate the grieving process.

When the time is right, survivors will begin to enjoy life again. Healing does occur.

Many survivors find that the best help comes from attending a support group for survivors of suicide where they can openly share their own story and their feelings with fellow survivors without pressure or fear of judgment and shame. Support groups can be a helpful source of guidance and understanding as well as a support in the healing process.

Children as Survivors

It is a myth that children don't grieve. Children may experience the same range of feelings as do adults; the expression of that grief might be different as children have fewer tools for communicating their feelings.

Children are especially vulnerable to feelings of guilt and abandonment. It is important for them to know that the death was not their fault and that someone is there to take care of them.

Secrecy about the suicide in the hopes of protecting children may cause further complications. Explain the situation and answer children's questions honestly and with age-appropriate responses.

American Association of Suicidology

The American Association of Suicidology (AAS) offers a variety of resources and programs to survivors in an attempt to lessen the pain as they travel their special path of grief. These include:

- Survivors of Suicide Kit: an information kit consisting of fact sheets, a bibliography and sample literature.
- *Survivors of Suicide: Coping with the Suicide of a Loved One* booklet and *A Handbook for Survivors of Suicide.*
- *Surviving Suicide*, a quarterly newsletter for survivors and survivor support groups.
- "Healing After Suicide", an annual conference held every April, for and about survivors.
- Suicide Prevention and Survivors of Suicide Resource Catalog: a listing of books, pamphlets, etc. which can be ordered from AAS. Includes resources for children and those who care for them.
- Directory of Survivors of Suicide Support Groups – print version available for purchase and an online version available at www.suicidology.org.
- Guidelines for Survivors of Suicide Support Groups: a how-to booklet on starting a support group.

The goal of the American Association of Suicidology (AAS) is to understand and prevent suicide. AAS promotes research, public awareness programs, education, and training for professionals, survivors, and all interested persons. AAS serves as a national clearinghouse for information on suicide. AAS has many resources and publications which are available to its membership and the general public. For membership information, please contact:

American Association of Suicidology
5221 Wisconsin Ave. N. W.
Washington, DC 20015
(202) 237-2280
(202) 237-2282 (Fax)
Email: info@suicidology.org
Website: www.suicidology.org

Additional Resources

- American Foundation for Suicide Prevention (AFSP) (www.afsp.org).
- Survivors of Suicide (www.survivorsofsuicide.com).
- The Link National Resource Center (www.thelink.org).

AMERICAN ASSOCIATION OF SUICIDOLOGY

Dedicated to the Understanding and Prevention of Suicide

Helping Survivors of Suicide: What Can You Do?

The loss of a loved one by suicide is often shocking, painful and unexpected. The grief that ensues can be intense, complex and long term. Grief and bereavement are an extremely individual and unique process.

There is no given duration to being bereaved by suicide. Survivors of suicide are not looking for their lives to return to their prior state because things can never go back to how they were. Survivors aim to adjust to life without their loved one.

Common emotions experienced with grief are:

Shock	Denial
Pain	Numbness
Anger	Shame
Dispair	Disbelief
Depression	Stress
Sadness	Guilt
Rejection	Loneliness
Abandonment	Anxiety

The single most important and helpful thing you can do as a friend is <u>listen</u>. Actively listen, without judgment, criticism, or prejudice, to what the survivor is telling you. Because of the stigma surrounding suicide, survivors are often hesitant to openly share their story and express their feelings. In order to help, you must overcome any preconceptions you have about suicide and the suicide victim. This is best accomplished by educating yourself about suicide. While you may feel uncomfortable discussing suicide and its aftermath, survivor loved ones are in great pain and in need of your compassion.

Ask the survivor if and how you can help. They may not be ready to share and may want to grieve privately before accepting help.

Let them talk at their own pace; they will share with you when (and what) they are ready to.

Be patient. Repetition is a part of healing, and as such you may hear the same story multiple times. Repetition is part of the healing process and survivors need to tell their story as many times as is necessary.

Use the loved one's name instead of 'he' or 'she'. This humanizes the decedent; the use of the decedent's name will be comforting.

You may not know what to say, and that's okay. Your presence and unconditional listening is what a survivor is looking for.

You cannot lead someone through their grief. The journey is personal and unique to the individual. Do not tell them how they should act, what they should feel, or that they should feel better "by now".

Avoid statements like "I know how you feel"; unless you are a survivor, you can only empathize with how they feel.

August 20, 2004

Survivors of suicide support groups are helpful to survivors to express their feelings, tell their story, and share with others who have experienced a similar event. These groups are good resources for the healing process and many survivors find them helpful. Please consult our website (www.suicidology.org) for a listing of support groups in or near your community.

The American Association of Suicidology (AAS) offers a variety of resources and programs to survivors in an attempt to lessen the pain as they travel their special path of grief. These include:

- Survivors of Suicide Kit: an information kit consisting of fact sheets, a bibliography, and sample literature.
- *Survivors of Suicide: Coping with the Suicide of a Loved One* booklet and *A Handbook for Survivors of Suicide.*
- *Surviving Suicide*, a quarterly newsletter for survivors and survivor support groups.
- "Healing After Suicide", an annual conference held every April, for and about survivors.
- Suicide Prevention and Survivors of Suicide Resource Catalog: a listing of books, pamphlets, etc. which can be ordered from AAS. Includes resources for children and those who care for them.
- Directory of Survivors of Suicide Support Groups – print version available for purchase and an online version available at www.suicidology.org.
- Guidelines for Survivors of Suicide Support Groups: a how-to booklet on starting a support group.

Additional Resources

- Survivors of Suicide (www.survivorsofsuicide.com).
- Suicide Awareness: Voices of Education (SAVE) (www.save.org).
- American Foundation for Suicide Prevention (AFSP) (www.afsp.org).

American Association of Suicidology

The goal of the American Association of Suicidology (AAS) is to understand and prevent suicide. AAS promotes research, public awareness programs, education, and training for professionals, survivors, and all interested persons. AAS serves as a national clearinghouse for information on suicide. AAS has many resources and publications, which are available to its membership and the general public. For membership information, please contact:

American Association of Suicidology
5221 Wisconsin Ave. N. W.
Washington, DC 20015
(202) 237-2280
(202) 237-2282 (Fax)
Email: info@suicidology.org
Website: www.suicidology.org

International Journal of Emergency Mental Health, Vol. 7, No. 2, pp. 133-140 © 2005 Chevron Publishing ISSN 1522-4821

Enhancing the Crisis Management Briefing

Daniel W. Clark
Washington State Patrol

Peter Volkmann
Town of Ossining, NY Police Department

ABSTRACT: *The Crisis Management Briefing (CMB) is a powerful and versatile crisis intervention tool, effective within a wide variety of populations, settings, and critical incidents. Initially proposed by Everly (2000), the CMB uniquely fills the factual information void following a critical incident. Additionally, a CMB provides essential information on effective coping strategies and available helping resources, tailored to the specific incident(s). The authors expand on the original CMB construct using their combined field experience, offering recommendations on team composition, strategic planning factors, using CISDs vs. CMBs, and specific enhancements for the four phases. They conclude with examples of specific interventions across a variety of events to illustrate their recommendations. [International Journal of Emergency Mental Health, 2005, 7(2), pp. 133-140].*

KEY WORDS: *crisis intervention, Crisis Management Briefing, Critical Incident Stress Management, traumatic stress, suicide, disaster, strategic planning*

Enhancing the Crisis Management Briefing

Crisis intervention techniques developed out of disaster and military writings beginning in the early 1900s. Mitchell and Everly applied these established crisis intervention strategies to high-risk/high-exposure populations such as public safety and emergency responders in the 1980s. This support program for emergency personnel has been refined and expanded into the current multicomponent Critical Incident Stress Management (CISM) system over the past 20 years (Everly & Mitchell, 1999; Flannery & Everly, 2000; Mitchell, 2003).

Daniel W. Clark, Ph.D., Washington State Patrol; Peter Volkmann, LMSW, Town of Ossining, NY Police Department. The authors would like to thank Dr. Jeffrey Lating for his valuable suggestions in the preparation and editing of this article. Correspondence concerning this article should be addressed to Daniel W. Clark, Ph.D., Washington State Patrol, 1405 Harrison Avenue NW, Suite 205, Olympia, Washington, 98502. Telephone number (360) 586-8492, fax number (360) 664-0356. Electronic mail may be sent to wsp-psych@att.net.

Conceptually, CISM is an integrated system of ten crisis intervention tools or core elements, such as peer support, Critical Incident Stress Debriefings (CISD), defusings, pre-incident education, and Crisis Management Briefings. These tools, applied appropriately and within the scope of design by trained individuals, are effective in assisting individuals and groups in crisis (Bohl, 1991, 1995; Chemtob, Tomas, Law, & Cremniter, 1997; Flannery, 2001; Richards, 2001; Wee, Mills, & Koehler, 1999).

The Crisis Management Briefing (CMB), one of the most recently developed CISM interventions, is a powerful and versatile tool that CISM practitioners need to know. Everly (2000) described the CMB as "...a group psychological crisis intervention designed to mitigate the levels of felt crisis and traumatic stress in the wake of terrorism, mass disasters, violence, and other large scale crises (p.53)."

Few reports discuss using CMBs as large group interventions; however, Castellano (2003) reported modifying the CMB format, and pairing it with a CISD in a 2-day intervention for law enforcement officers following the tragic events of September 11, 2001. Sheehan, Everly, & Langlieb (2004) recommend large group crisis interventions as one of five core competencies in a best practices model for coping with major critical incidents.

The authors have successfully used CMBs for the past several years. Our field experience suggests the CMB is effective across many situations. The authors have used CMBs following aviation incidents/accidents, suicides of co-workers, officer involved shootings, line of duty deaths, serious motor vehicle accidents, school crisis responses, and corporate crisis responses.

In this article, we will review the CMB as originally presented, contrast CISDs with CMBs, and then expand the framework introduced in Everly's 2000 article with "back pocket" practical skills. We conclude with specific examples from our experiences.

The Original CMB

The CMB is an efficient, large group intervention with primary goals of providing information, controlling rumors, reducing a sense of chaos, offering coping resources, and facilitating referrals to the mental health system. In addition, a CMB facilitates follow-up care, assesses further needs of the group, and can stimulate increased group cohesion and morale (Everly, 2000).

A CMB is a four-phase group intervention typically lasting 30-75 minutes. The original target audience was primary victim civilian populations following mass disasters, terrorism, violence, and large-scale crises. CMBs may be scheduled any time post-crisis, and may be repeated multiple times.

The first phase (Assembly) gathers those affected by the incident in order to reestablish a sense of community. The second phase (Fact) provides accurate and factual information regarding the incident that evoked the CMB. In the third phase (Reactions), a credible healthcare professional or mental health professional (MHP) presents common signs, symptoms, and psychological themes relevant to the incident. The final phase (Teaching) focuses on providing personal coping and self-care strategies, practical stress management techniques, and options for professional referral and follow-up.

Strategic Planning Factors

Strategic planning is a process which yields a set of decisions about how, why, and what to do (What is strategic planning?, 1999). Within CISM, this means selecting the right set of CISM interventions, applying them at the right time, with the right resources. CISM teams need to consider: the Target population which needs assistance, the Timing of these interventions so as to be most helpful, the Resources required to provide the best services to those in need, and the Type(s) of intervention which best fit the situation, (Everly & Mitchell, 1999; Mitchell, 2004)

Target population

We have found CMBs to be extremely useful with a variety of audiences, including civilians, military personnel, and emergency responders. Group size may vary from 10-300.

Timing

CMBs may be scheduled anytime following the critical incident. Consider scheduling multiple CMBs to better accommodate family care and shift work needs. For instance, schedule one CMB during business hours, another in the evening, and perhaps another on the weekend to provide those affected several opportunities to attend.

In addition, during a prolonged incident, sequential CMBs can update factual or operational information as well as present information on specific reactions and coping strategies.

Resources/team members

The CISM team composition will vary from incident to incident. Although the Everly (2000) article does not specifically address team composition, we offer the following recommendations.

First, recruit a knowledgeable and respected spokesperson to explain the facts of the situation, such as the police chief, mayor, school superintendent, or disaster coordinator. Second, use a credible healthcare professional or a mental health professional to address common reactions to the incident. Third, use a peer, a Chaplain, or a MHP to address personal coping and practical self-care strategies. Our exprience suggests it is particularly effective to use a peer with "been there, done that" experience for this last phase.

Finally, we have found it effective to position trained peer supporters throughout the audience. Peer supporters can play a crucial role in gathering information both before and during the first phase (discussed below). Additionally, trained peer supporters can be available for individual interventions once the formal CMB is completed. The number of peer supporters needed will vary depending on the severity of the incident. During a CMB for a completed suicide, for example, the authors recommend one peer per 5-8 expected attendees. For a CMB following a large-scale event, the authors recommend one peer per 15-20 expected attendees.

Essentially, the CMB may be effective any time, with any group involved in a critical incident.

Type of intervention - CISD vs. CMB

Determining which Type(s) of intervention to use is a vital part of strategic planning. Although CISDs and CMBs are fundamentally different tools, both apply established crisis intervention principles. Crisis intervention has been described as psychological first aid, the goals of which are stabilization, mitigation of acute signs and symptoms of distress, restoration of independent functioning, and facilitation of access to higher levels of care (Everly, 2003; Everly & Mitchell, 2000; Flannery & Everly, 2000; Mitchell, 2003).

The goals of a CISD include facilitating psychological closure of the event, mitigating symptoms, and performing triage, as necessary. Participants are encouraged to share their thoughts and reactions to a critical incident during a 1-3 hour group process. CISDs are typically scheduled 24-72 hours post-event but may occur up to 10 days later or even longer following a large disaster or incidents such as September 11th. CISM debriefing teams are designed to include a MHP and at least one peer (see Table 1).

The goals of a CMB are to provide information about the incident, plus offer psychological consultation and stress management information. A CISM team presents this information to the assembled group in a panel format scheduled anytime post-crisis. The team may be composed of MHPs, Chaplains, and/or peers. Conceptually, the intent of a CISD is to "pull" reactions from the group, while the intent of a CMB is to "push" information to the group.

In general, the decision to offer CISM interventions should be based on the psychological needs of the target group and their readiness to begin the healing process. If the participants want to talk about a critical incident, particularly if the participants are emergency responders or military personnel, a CISD may be the better choice. Jacobs, Horne-Moyer, and Jones (2004) found that CISDs are effective for reducing risk for PTSD-related symptoms in emergency ser-

Table 1.
Contrasting CISDs and CMBs

	CISD	**CMB**
Goals	Facilitate closure,symptom mitigation,triage	Inform about incident,psychological consultation,stress management
Intent	"Pull" reactions	"Push" information
Group size	Small groups	Small to large groups
When	1-10 days post-crisis (or longer in disasters)	Anytime post-crisis, may be repeated
Team composition	Mental health professional (MHP) plus peers, Chaplains	MHP, peer, or Chaplain plus spokesperson
Length	1-3 hours	15-75 minutes
Follow-up	Closure, referral	Assess need for CISD, individual crisis interventions, referral

vices personnel, more so than for primary victim populations.

If the participants primarily want information about an event, or if they are not emergency responders or military personnel, consider offering a CMB. After conducting a CMB, if participants want an opportunity to talk about the event as a group, consider holding a CISD as a follow-up intervention.

Additional factors to consider in choosing to use a CMB include:

1) Does the CISM team have limited knowledge of individual levels of traumatization within the affected group?
2) Is the group large and not readily split into smaller groups, such as in a line of duty death incident?
3) Is there a high probability for litigation for the participants or the department, such as following an officer involved shooting?
4) Would detailed description of incident details by some participants traumatize other participants?

Certain incidents may require limited interaction between affected personnel due to pending litigation. The CMB's design limits participant interaction with one another during the intervention. If the CISM Team determines that limiting interaction between participants may be beneficial, the CMB may be the appropriate intervention for the group.

Crisis Management Briefings: Recommended Enhancements

Team Pre-meeting

Although not a formal phase in the CMB, prior to any CISM group intervention, the CISM team needs to properly plan the upcoming intervention. Be aware that some CISM team members, peers and MHPs alike, may lack training in this core element because the CMB is CISM's newest group intervention. Note, however, Mitchell (2004) and a National Institutes of Mental Health report (NIMH, 2002) both stress the importance of using only properly trained team members to provide crisis intervention.

During this team meeting, designate the roles of each CISM member, assign primary duties per phase, and determine which team members will check with anyone who leaves the CMB early. Also, interview the person who will give the facts of the incident. A "fact giver" or a facts spokesperson is necessary because the CISM team does not investigate the incident nor do they have the credibility to provide the facts of what happened.

The choice of the spokesperson for the facts phase is critical. A senior, respected, and credible person is ideal. For example, if the incident is a serious accident involving an emergency responder, the Chief or senior member of the organization may be the most appropriate fact giver. In a prolonged situation, perhaps a lead investigator would be best. In a community incident such as a flood, perhaps the mayor or senior local relief official may be most appropriate. In a school-based incident, the principal or district superintendent would likely be the logical choice. Bottom line, the spokesperson must have accurate and factual information, and be able to understand and effectively convey this information.

This person is *not* likely to be CISM trained. We recommend giving this spokesperson an outline of what you would like them to cover, and explain how the factual information complements the remainder of the CMB. For instance, in the serious accident scenario suggested above, prepare the spokesperson to address the facts of what happened, as currently known. If there will be a source for continuing information on the incident, e.g. a web site or phone number, ask the spokesperson to share this as well.

Certain personality types, such as uncompromising or overly quiet types, may not be the best choice for the Facts Phase spokesperson particularly when the group requires empathic understanding. The team must ensure the spokesperson is comfortable providing facts to this group and understands the material he/she will present during Phase II, Facts. Some teams may have no choice regarding the person providing the facts, and will need to anticipate that this person may incite negative reactions in this group in crisis, e.g., an unpopular elected official or someone perceived as non-supportive of the emergency services.

A final note regarding the facts spokesperson: he or she may need reminding that this is *not* an opportunity to make political comments or to further personal agendas. The team may need to help the spokesperson focus on the crisis response aspect of the CMB.

We cannot stress enough the importance of this team pre-meeting. In our experience, without this team meeting, the likelihood of a successful and effective CMB decreases.

Phase I, Assembly

This phase was originally the first step in assisting the group in reestablishing a sense of community. The power of group support is important to individuals in crisis, enforcing the idea that "we are in this together."

We recommend also using this time to gather additional information. Team members mingle with the group as it assembles to assess the stress reactions and emotions of the group, listening and gently probing for current concerns and questions. The team members then relay this information to the team members responsible for Phases III and IV, allowing those team members to address these concerns during their remarks. This allows the team to present common signs and reactions while also teaching personal stress skills appropriate to this group in crisis.

This phase also allows the CISM team to assess which individuals are receiving support and which have been cast away from the group. Mental health professionals observe healthy and unhealthy group dynamics. Potential target groups and individuals may be identified for follow up and possible referral.

Phase II, Facts

This is a crucial phase of the CMB. People often seek accurate and factual information following a critical incident. We typically want to understand what happened, and why it happened, if possible. Knowing the facts helps reduce anticipatory anxiety and returns a sense of control to those impacted by the event (Flannery & Everly, 2000; Mitchell & Everly, 2001). It is important to emphasize that the information presented is the best available at this time, and is subject to change. The CISM team will answer questions from attendees at the completion of Phase IV.

This phase is also where the spokesperson addresses any rumors through providing accurate, factual information. The spokesperson may simply state the investigation is ongoing and there are no definitive conclusions.

The spokesperson does not answer questions posed after the group receives the facts. This prevents the CMB from bogging down with audience questions about the facts. The group may need reminding that the CISM team will address their questions after providing personal coping and stress management information.

Phase III, Reactions

This phase is similar to the initial half of the Teaching Phase of a Critical Incident Stress Debriefing. A credible, CISM trained healthcare professional or MHP presents common signs, symptoms, and psychological themes relevant to the incident.

Common signs and symptoms might include reactions such as anger, grief, fear, uncertainty, poor concentration, nightmares, and survivor guilt, depending on the incident. Attendees may also be experiencing sleep and appetite changes, relationship difficulties, hypervigilance, social withdrawal, intolerance of others, fatigue, etc. (Everly & Mitchell, 1999; Mitchell & Everly, 2003).

Psychological themes will be incident specific. For example, following an incident where an officer is severely injured or killed on a "routine" traffic stop, other officers may find themselves less willing to initiate traffic stops and more aware of their own mortality. Following a suicide, psychological themes typically include the guilt and anger the survivors are feeling, as well as concern for the soul of the deceased.

This phase is where the information the peers gathered prior to and during Phase I becomes important. The healthcare or mental health professional can use the general symptoms and themes listed above for common reactions, but the CMB can be even more effective if the team addresses the specific concerns, reactions, or fears of the attendees. Judicious use of the CISM phrase, "a normal reaction of normal people to abnormal events," is likely to be helpful here.

Phase IV, Teaching

This phase is similar to the latter half of the Teaching Phase of a CISD. A CISM trained peer, Chaplain, or MHP may lead the phase. The focus is on providing personal coping and self-care strategies, practical stress management techniques, and referral information. These recommendations need to fit the incident as much as possible.

Common recommendations include maintaining as normal a schedule as possible, getting plenty of rest, eating well-balanced and regular meals, exercising to reduce physical stress, and avoiding the use of alcohol to relax. In addition, we recommend talking to other people "because talking can be very healing." Another valuable recommendation is encouraging attendees to remember and apply stress reduction techniques that have worked for them before. We also suggest the attendees share these recommendations with family and significant others (Bolton, Glenn, Orsillo, Roemer, & Linz, 2003; Clark & Haley, in press; Flannery, 2004; Mitchell & Everly, 2003).

We strongly encourage local CISM teams to provide reference sheets covering the material presented in Phases III and IV. These sheets should cover signs and symptoms, common reactions, coping strategies, and local professional referral sources. As an example, in the back of the CISM: Group Crisis Intervention workbook are two pages listing common reactions on one side and coping strategies on the reverse (Mitchell & Everly, 2003, p. 137-138). We encourage taking the information presented on those two pages and customizing it for individual teams. One of the authors printed the information using a tri-fold format on card stock, and added contact numbers for the CISM team as an additional resource (see http://www.criticalconcepts.org/Downloads.htm/ for examples).

If the attendees have questions, we recommend answering the questions following the completion of Phase IV. However, know the limitations of your knowledge and *never* go beyond those limitations. If you do not know something, say so. If you do not know but can find out, say so. Be very wary of promising information you cannot deliver. Remember, one of the core goals in a CMB is to provide accurate, factual information in order to dispel rumors.

The length of a CMB is generally 30-75 minutes, although individual crisis interventions typically offered by trained interventionists on a voluntary basis following the conclusion of the CMB may continue for an extended time. The severity of the incident prompting the CMB appears to determine the duration of the CMB, with more severe incidents generally requiring longer CMBs.

This concludes the formal portion of the CMB. However, be prepared for attendees to stay an additional 30 minutes or more, talking amongst themselves in small groups and with the peer supporters placed throughout the audience. In fact, we recommend you encourage this behavior by providing light refreshments in the back of the room at the conclusion of the CMB. Simple trays of fruits or vegetables, crackers or pretzels, and bottled water or soft drinks are sufficient.

We have learned that if you provide food, most people will stay and eat the food, giving the CISM team another opportunity to interact with the attendees.

Examples

One of the authors worked with two air ambulance companies following separate accidents, one with fatalities among the flight crew. In both cases, the CISM team chose to conduct a CMB in the morning and follow-up with a CISD that same afternoon. During the CMB, the focus was on giving the assembled employees factual information about the accident. We recruited the senior pilot and/or the safety officer for Phase II (Facts), the author spoke during Phase III (Reactions), and an experienced, senior flight nurse spoke during Phase IV (Teaching).

The feedback we received was very positive. The combination of providing specific technical information related to the accident, then allowing those who attended the CISD to process their reactions to both the accident and the factual information appeared to be very beneficial.

A second example from one author's experience suggests using the CMB as a post-suicide CISM intervention is very helpful, especially in conjunction with CISDs, family interventions, and individual crisis interventions. Following a suicide, the suicide survivors (those who knew the individual) actively question why this suicide occurred. Due in part to the lack of factual information and the high emotions following this type of critical incident, many rumors circulate.

Following an officer suicide, one of the authors scheduled several CMBs. The local District Commander presented Phase II (Facts), and the author spoke during Phase III (Reactions) and Phase IV (Teaching). Trained peer supporters provided individual crisis interventions following completion of the formal CMB.

Using the CMB to distribute accurate and factual information, normalizing common reactions such as guilt, anger, and loss, and presenting effective coping strategies provided a powerful service. The majority of the time, we find the formal portion of the CMB lasts 30-45 minutes but the informal peer support and individual crisis interventions may last an additional 30 minutes or more.

Finally, the authors' experience suggests modifying CMBs for roll calls or shift changes. Shift change briefings in emergency services, usually limited to approximately 15 minutes, consist of passing factual information to the oncoming shift. A CMB can follow that customary factual format, plus normalize reactions, and provide personal stress management tools and resources available for support.

The shortened shift change CMB remains a four-step process. Phase I, Assembly, has already occurred. Phase II, Facts, addresses the facts of the incident(s). Phase III, Reactions, is a quick listing of possible reactions to the incident(s). A handout of available resources and coping strategies replaces Phase IV, Teaching. The Q&A is limited to a few questions. One on one informal discussions occur after the shift change briefing as personnel move to their assigned posts.

Future research

This paper represents the authors' clinical anecdotal evidence for the effectiveness of CMBs. The next logical step is conducting empirical research studies designed to support the authors' experience. A potential design might include questionnaires administered pre- and post-CMB regarding perceived change in affect, reactions, locus of control, etc. Questions also could be included in the post-CMB form asking about the perceived effectiveness of this intervention.

An important point to consider is Jacobs, Horne-Moyer, and Jones' (2004) conclusion that CISDs may be an effective means of reducing risk for PTSD-related symptoms in emergency responders, but may be less effective when applied to primary victims – those actually involved in the critical incidents. Therefore, an appropriate research question may be "with whom are CMBs effective," rather than "are CMBs effective?"

Conclusions

One of the voids following any critical incident is the availability of accurate and factual information. The CMB uniquely fills the factual information void as well as provides critical information on effective coping strategies and available helping resources. It is a robust tool, flexible enough to be effective with a wide variety of populations, settings, and critical incidents.

Strategic planning and assessment of the situation are key to providing proper interventions. CISM teams must carefully consider and select the most appropriate elements to use given the composition of the affected group, the incident itself, the available resources, and the timeline.

The authors have shared their experiences with the CMB, and provided their thoughts on expanding the CMB concept in scope and application from its original formulation. We highly recommend the effectiveness and the utility of the CMB format, particularly when used in conjunction with other CISM interventions.

REFERENCES

Bohl, N. (1991). The effectiveness of brief psychological interventions in police officers after critical incidents. In J.T.Reese, J. Horn, and C. Dunning (Eds.) *Critical Incidents in Policing, Revised* (pp. 31-38). Washington, DC: Department of Justice.

Bohl, N. (1995). Measuring the effectiveness of CISD. *Fire Engineering, 148*(8) 125-126.

Bolton, E.E., Glenn, D.M., Orsillo, S., Roemer, L. and Linz, B.T. (2003). The relationship between self-disclosure and symptoms of posttraumatic stress disorder in peacekeepers deployed to Somalia. *Journal of Traumatic Stress, 16* (3), 203-210.

Castellano, C. (2003). Large group crisis intervention for law enforcement in response to the September 11 World Trade Center Mass Disaster. *International Journal of Emergency Mental Health, 5*(4), 211-215.

Chemtob, C.M., Tomas, S., Law, W., and Cremniter, D. (1997). Postdisaster psychosocial intervention: A field study of the impact of debriefing on psychological distress. *American Journal of Psychiatry, 154*(3), 415-417.

Clark, D.W. and Haley, M. (in press). Crisis response tools for law enforcement. *Police Chief.*

Everly Jr., G.S. (2000). Crisis Management Briefings (CMB): Large group crisis intervention in response to terrorism, disasters, and violence. *International Journal of Emergency Mental Health, 2*(1), 53-57.

Everly Jr., G.S. (2003). Early psychological intervention: A word of caution. *International Journal of Emergency Mental Health, 5*(4), 179-184.

Everly Jr., G.S. and Mitchell, J. (1999). *Critical Incident Stress Management (CISM): A New Era and Standard of Care in Crisis Intervention* (2nd ed.). Ellicott City, MD: Chevron Publishing.

Everly Jr., G.S. and Mitchell, J. (2000). The Debriefing "Controversy" and crisis intervention: A review of lexical and substantive issues. *International Journal of Emergency Mental Health, 2*(4), 211-225.

Flannery Jr., R.B. and Everly, Jr. G.S. (2000). Crisis intervention: A review. *International Journal of Emergency Mental Health, 2*(2), 119-125.

Flannery Jr., R.B. (2001). Assaulted Staff Action Program (ASAP): Ten years of empirical support for Critical Incident Stress Management. *International Journal of Emergency Mental Health, 3*(1), 5-10.

Flannery Jr., R.B. (2004). Managing stress in today's age: A concise guide for emergency services personnel. *International Journal of Emergency Mental Health, 6*(4), 205-209.

Jacobs, J., Horne-Moyer, H.L., and Jones, R. (2004). The effectiveness of Critical Incident Stress Debriefing with primary and secondary trauma victims. *International Journal of Emergency Mental Health, 6*(1), 5-14.

National Institutes of Mental Health (2002). *Mental Health and Mass Violence: Evidence-Based Early Psychological Intervention for Victims / Survivors of Mass Violence. A Workshop to Reach Consensus on Best Practices.* NIH Publication No. 02-5138, Washington, D.C.: U.S. Government Printing Office.

Mitchell, J.T. (2003). Major misconceptions in crisis intervention. *International Journal of Emergency Mental Health, 5*(4), 185-197.

Mitchell, J.T. (2004). Characteristics of successful early intervention programs. *International Journal of Emergency Mental Health, 6*(4), 175-184.

Mitchell, J.T. and Everly Jr., G.S. (2003). Critical Incident Stress Management (CISM): Group crisis intervention. (3rd ed. Rev.). Ellicott City, MD: International Critical Incident Stress Foundation.

Richards, D. (2001). A field study of critical incident stress debriefing versus critical incident stress management. *Journal of Mental Health, 10*(3), 351-362.

Sheehan, D.C., Everly Jr., G.S., and Langlieb, A. (2004). Current best practices: Coping with major critical incidents. *FBI Law Enforcement Bulletin, 73*(9), 1-13.

Wee, D.F., Mills, D.M., and Koehler, G. (1999). The effects of Critical Incident Stress Debriefing on emergency medical services personnel following the Los Angeles civil disturbance. *International Journal of Emergency Mental Health, 1*(1), 33-38.

"What is strategic planning?" (1999). Retrieved January 11, 2005, from http://www.nonprofits.org/npofaq/03/22.html.

Post Action Staff Support (PASS): Operational Guidelines
Dennis Potter, LMSW and Paul LaBerteaux, PsyD

WHY DO IT?

When a CISM team has finished it's work with the personnel involved in a Critical Incident, they are normally tired and ready to return to their own lives. However, they still have one piece of work left to be done, namely to take a few minutes to take care of themselves. Because they have spent several hours being exposed to the pain of the personnel involved in the event, they too have become participants in it. As a result, members of the CISM team may be having some reactions to the CISM response. We need to take care of ourselves! We suggest that PASS might be a model that would be helpful.

Through the process of PASS, you are working to accomplish three goals:

- You are attempting to **prevent** negative reactions such as vicarious traumatization, cumulative stress and the effects of negative self judgment.
- You are using this as an opportunity to **teach and reinforce skills** demonstrated during the CISM response.
- You are "**practicing what we preach**" to personnel in the debriefing!

By assuring that PASS is a standard operating procedure for your team, you are increasing their effectiveness and longevity on the team. You are decreasing the chances for any negative personal reactions by members of the team and monitoring the team for any adverse reactions. Lastly, like you did for the participants in the CISM activities, you are preparing the CISM team for re-entry into the world.

Normally the PASS should be done shortly after their work is done and before the team separates to go home. If a team has been involved in a particularly difficult response or a series of defusings/debriefings/demobilizations over a prolonged event response, the PASS might better be done within a few days. This will allow the team an opportunity to process some of the event on their own and then to finish the work together.

The PASS process normally takes 15 to 30 minutes for "regular" CISM activities and longer for particularly difficult or long responses.

WHO SHOULD DO IT?

Usually the team leader or an experienced peer can lead the PASS process. Again, if the CISM team has been through a particularly difficult or long response, their PASS is best accomplished by someone who was not a direct part of the activities. This allows all team members to participate in the full experience of the PASS process.

HOW DO YOU DO IT?

The Post Action Staff Support process uses a variation of the CISD. It consists of three phases, REVIEW, RESPONSE, and REMIND.

The REVIEW phase is essentially a combination of the Introduction/Fact/Thought phase of the regular CISD. It utilizes questions designed to have members think about and discuss the CISM activities and their participation in it. The following questions are examples of this phase:

- How did it go?
- How do you think you did?
- What "ditzy" thing did you do?
- What themes emerged?
- What was the participation level of the group?

During this phase, the leader can guide the discussion into teaching what made the CISM response go well or give examples of other ways to have handled some aspect of the activities.

The RESPONSE phase is a condensation of the Reaction/Symptom phase of the CISD and works to elicit comments on the self perception of the team members and any concerns they may have about their performance. The following types of questions seem to work well:

- What did you say that you wish you hadn't?
- What didn't you say that you wish you had?
- How has this debriefing affected you?
- What is the hardest part of this debriefing for you?

During this phase, the leader guides some group discussion of the members self perceptions. What usually follows is reassurance by the team members that no major errors occurred. This is also an opportunity for the team leader and team members to reassure each other that each individual contributed to the process and to offer alternative methods for handling problem issues.

The REMIND phase correlates to the Teaching/Re-entry phase of the CISD. Questions in this step serve to help the team remember to do the same sort of things that we encourage the debriefees to do.

- Is there any follow up to be done?
- What are you going to do to take care of yourself in the next 24 hours?
- What will it take for you to "let go" of this debriefing?

By using this structured approach to a PASS, CISM teams are maximizing the opportunities for teaching members new skills, minimizing the chances for members returning home distressed or full of self doubt and assuring its members that they are valuable assets to the team. Being involved in a CISM team ought to be a rewarding experience for all team members it is our responsibility to take care of ourselves at least as well as we try to take care of others.

If we believe in what we are doing for the individuals we serve, we should believe in what we are doing for the individuals providing the services!

SECTION FIVE

Resources

Bibliography

Bullman, T. & Kang, H. (1996). The risk of suicide among wounded Vietnam veterans. *American Journal of Public Health, 86*(5), 662-667.

Canapary, D., Bongar, B., and Cleary, K. (2002) Assessing risk for completed suicide in patients with alcohol dependence: Clinicans' views of critical factors. *Professional Psychology, Research and Practice, 33*(5), 464-469.

Clark, D.W. & White, E.K. (2003). Cops, clinicians, and suicide. In D.P. Hackett & J.M. Violanti (Eds.). *Police suicide: Tactics for prevention* (pp. 16-36). Springfield: Thomas.

Covey, Stephen R (1989). *The seven habits of highly effective people.* New York: Simon and Schuster.

Ferrada-Noli, M., Asberg M., and Ormstad K. (1998). Suicidal behavior after severe trauma. Part 2: The association between methods of torture and of suicidal ideation in posttraumatic stress disorder. *Journal of Traumatic Stress. 11*(1), 113-24.

Hendin, H. and Haas, A. (1991). Suicide and guilt as manifestations of PTSD in Vietnam combat veterans. *American Journal of Psychiatry, 148*, 586-591.

Janik, J. and Kravitz, H. (1994). Police suicides: Trouble at home. In J.T. Reese & E. Scrivner (Eds.), *Law Enforcement Families: Issues and Answers* (pp.73-81). U.S. Government Printing.

Jordan, J. (2001). Is suicide bereavement different? A reassessment of the literature. *Suicide and Life-Threatening Behavior, 31*(1), 91-102.

Kisch, J., Leino, V., and Silverman, M.M. (2005). Aspects of suicidal behavior, depression, and treatment in college students: Results from the Spring 2000 National College Health Assessment Survey. *Suicide and Life-Threatening Behavior, 35*(1), 3-13.

Kneiper, A. (1999). The suicide survivor's grief and recovery. *Suicide and Life-Threatening Behavior, 29*(4), 353-364.

Krug, Etienne G.; Kresnow, Marcie-jo; Peddicord, John P.; Dahlberg, Linda L.; Powell, Kenneth E.; Crosby, Alex E.; Annest, Joseph L. (1998). Suicide after Natural Disasters. *New England Journal of Medicine, 338,* 373-8.

Kubler-Ross, E. (1969). *On death and dying*. New York: Macmillian.

Loo, R. (2001). Effective Postvention for Police Suicide. *The Australian Journal of Disaster and Trauma Studies*. Vol 2001-2.

Luoma, J.B., Martin, C.E., and Pearson, J.L. (2002). Contact with mental health and primary care providers before suicide: A review of the evidence. *American Journal of Psychiatry, 159,* 909-916.

National Strategy for Suicide Prevention. *Suicide: Cost to the nation.* www.mentalhealth.org.

Nossiter, Adam. (2005, 27 December). Hurricane takes a further toll: Suicides up in New Orleans. *New York Times*. Retrieved January 1, 2006, from www.nytimes.com/.

Patterson, W., Dohn, H., Bird, J. and Patterson, G. (1983). Evaluation of suicidal patients: The SAD PERSONS scale. *Psychosomatics, 24*(4), 343-349.

Ramsay, J.R. & Newman, C.F. (2005). After the attempt: Maintaining the therapeutic alliance following a patient's suicide attempt. *Suicide and Life-Threatening Behavior, 35*(4), 413-424.

Shneidman, E.S. (1981). Postvention: The care of the bereaved. In E.S. Shneidman, *Suicide: Thoughts and reflections, 1960-1980* (pp. 157-167). New York: Human Sciences Press.

Shneidman, E. (1993). *Suicide as psychache: A clinical approach to self-destructive behavior.* Northvale, NJ: Jason Aronson.

Shneidman, E. (1987). A psychological approach to suicide. In A. Baum, C.J. Frederick, I.H. Frieze, E.S. Shneidman & C.B. Wortman (Eds.), *Cataclysms, crises, and catastrophes: Psychology in action* (pp. 147-183). Washington, D.C.: American Psychological Association.

SPAN USA, Inc. (2001). *Suicide Prevention: Prevention Effectiveness and Evaluation.* SPAN USA, Atlanta, GA.

Thompson, M., Kaslow, N., Kingree, J., Puett, R., Thompson, N. and Meadows, L. (1999). Partner abuse and Posttraumatic Stress Disorder as risk factors for suicide attempts in a sample of low-income, inner-city women. *Journal of Traumatic Stress, 12*(1), 59-71.

U.S. Public Health Service, *The Surgeon General's Call to Action to Prevent Suicide.* Washington DC: 1999.

General Suicide References

Bolton, Iris (1983). *My son, my son: A guide to healing after death, loss, or suicide.* Atlanta: Bolton Press.

Bongar, B., Berman, A.L., Maris, R.W., Silverman, M.M., Harris, E.A., & Packman, W.L. (Eds.). (1998). *Risk management with suicidal patients.* New York: Guilford.

Chance, Sue (1992). *Stronger than death: When suicide touches your life.* Bridgewater, NJ: Replica Books.

Mishara, Brian L. (Eds.) (1995). *The impact of suicide.* New York: Springer.

Pollock, L.R. & Williams, J.M.G. (1998). Problem solving and suicidal behavior. *Suicide and Life-Threatening Behavior, 28*(4), 375-387.

Shea, Shawn Christopher (1999). *The practical art of suicide assessment: A guide for mental health professionals and substance abuse counselors.* New York: Wiley & Sons.

Shneidman, Edwin (1993). *Suicide as Psychache: A clinical approach to self-destructive behavior.* Northvale, NJ: Jason Aronson.

Wrobleski, Adina (1995). *Suicide — why? 85 questions and answers about suicide.* Minneapolis, MN: Afterwords Pusblishing.

Wrobleski, Adina (2002). *Suicide survivors: A guide for those left behind.* Minneapolis, MN: SAVE, Suicide Awareness Voices of Education.

Contracts/No-Harm Contracts

Assey, J. L. (1985). The suicide prevention contract. *Perspectives in Psychiatric Care,* 3, 99-103.

Davidson, M.W., Wagner, W.G., & Range, L.M. (1995). Clinician's attitudes toward no-suicide agreements. *Suicide and Life Threatening Behavior, 25*(3), 410-414.

Egan, M. P. (1997). Contracting for safety: A concept analysis. *Crisis, 18/1,* 17-23.

Mahrer, J. & Bongar, B. (1993). Assessment and management of suicide risk and the use of the no-suicide contract. *Innovations in Clinical Practice: A Source Book, 12,* 277-293.

Miller, M. C., Jacobs, D. G., & Gutheil, T. G. (1998). Talisman or taboo: The controversy of the suicide-prevention contract. *Harvard Review of Psychiatry, 6*(2), 78-87.

Simon, R. I. (1999). The suicide prevention contract: Clinical, legal, and risk management issues. *Journal of the American Academy of Psychiatry and Law, 27*(3), 445-450.

Stanford, E. J., Goetz, R. R., & Bloom, J. D. (1994). The no harm contract in the emergency assessment of suicidal risk. *Journal of Clinical Psychiatry, 55*(8), 344-348.

Twiname, B. G. (1981). No-suicide contract for Nurses. *Journal of Psychiatric Nursing and Mental Health Services, 19*(7), 11-12.

Law enforcement suicide references

Allen, Scott W. (1986). Suicide and indirect self-destructive behavior among police. In *Psychological Services for Law Enforcement*, Edited by J.T. Reese & H.A. Goldstein, U.S. Government Printing, 413-417.

Baker, Thomas & Baker, Jane (1996). Preventing police suicide. *FBI Law Enforcement Bulletin, 65,* 24-27.

Clark, D.W. & White, E.K. (2000). Exploring law enforcement suicide: An inside look. Available at www.criticalconcepts.org/.

Clark, D.W. & White, E.K. (2003). Clinicians, cops, and suicide. In D.P. Hackett & J.M. Violanti (Eds.), *Police Suicide: Tactics for Prevention* (pp. 16-36). Springfield: Thomas.

Heiman, Michael F. (1977). Suicide among police. *American Journal of Psychiatry, 134*(11), 1286-1290.

Hem, E., Berg, A.M., & Ekeberg, O. (2001). Suicide in police – a critical review. *Suicide and Life Threatening Behavior, 31*(2), 224-233.

Honig, A.L. & White, E.K. (2000). By their own hand: Suicide among law enforcement personnel. *Police Chief, 67*(10), 156-160.

Quinnett, P. (July, 1998). QPR: Police suicide prevention, *FBI Law Enforcement Bulletin, 6* (7), 19-24.

Violanti, J.M. (1995). Trends in police suicides. *Psychological Reports, 77*(2), 688-690.

Violanti, J. (1995). The mystery within, understanding police suicide. *FBI Law Enforcement Bulletin, 64*, 19-23.

Violanti, J.M., Vena, J.E., Marshall, J.R., & Petralia, S. (1996). A comparative evaluation of police suicide rate validity. *Suicide and Life-Threatening Behavior, 26*(1), 79-85.

Violanti, J. (1996). *Police Suicide: Epidemic in Blue.* Springfield, IL: Thomas.

Wagner, M. & Brzeczek, R. (1983). Alcohol and suicide: A fatal connection. *FBI Law Enforcement Bulletin, 52,* 7-15.

Firefighter suicide references

Rawles, P. (2003). Not without warning. *Fire Chief,* April, 42-47.

Donaldson, V. & Donaldson, C. (1999). EMS hero commits suicide. *Journal of Emergency Medical Services, 24*(3), 94-100,103, 105.

Mitchell, J.T. (1995). Medic Suicide. What can be done? *Journal of Emergency Medical Services, 20*(11), 41-45.

Youth suicide references

Aseltine, R.H. & DeMartino, R. (2004). An outcome evaluation of the SOS Suicide Prevention Program. *American Journal of Public Health, 94*(3), 446-451.

Beautrais, A.L. (2003). Suicide and serious suicide attempts in youth: A multiple-group comparison study. *The American Journal of Psychiatry, 160,* 1093-1099.

Berman, A.L. & Jobes, D.A. (1995). Suicide prevention in adolescents. *Suicide and Life Threatening Behavior*, *25*(1), 143-154.

Brener, N.D., Krug, E.G., & Simon, T.R. (2000). Trends in suicide ideation and suicidal behavior among high school students in the United States, 1991-1997. *Suicide and Life Threatening Behavior, 30*(4), 304-313.

Gould, M.S. & Kramer, R.A. (2001). Youth suicide prevention. *Suicide and Life Threatening Behavior*, *31*(Suppl. 1), 6-31.

Hayden, D.C., & Lauer, P. (2000). Prevalence of suicide programs in schools and roadblocks to implementation. *Suicide and Life Threatening Behavior*, *30*(3), 239-251.

McEvoy, M.L., & McEvoy, A.W. (2000). *Preventing youth suicide.* Holmes Beach, FL: Learning Publications, Inc.

Leenaars, A.A. & Wenckstern, S. (1998). Principles of postvention: Applications to suicide and trauma in schools. *Death Studies, 22*, 357-391.

Lipschitz, D.S., Winegar, R.K., Nicolaou, A.L., Hartnick, E., Wolfson, M., & Southwick, S.M. (1999). Perceived abuse and neglect as risk factors for suicidal behavior in adolescent inpatients. *The Journal of Nervous and Mental Disease, 187*(1), 32-39.

Metha, A., Weber, B., & Webb, L.D. (1998). Youth suicide prevention: A survey and analysis of policies and efforts in the 50 states. *Suicide and Life Threatening Behavior*, *28*(2), 150-164.

Newman, Eileen. (2000). Group crisis intervention in a school setting following an attempted suicide. *International Journal of Emergency Mental Health*, *2*(2), 97-100.

Ramsay, J.R. & Newman, C.F. (2005). After the attempt: Maintaining the therapeutic alliance following a patient's suicide attempt. *Suicide and Life-Threatening Behavior*, *35*(4), 413-424.

Rathus, J.H. & Miller, A.L. (2002). Dialectical behavior therapy adapted for suicidal adolescents. *Suicide and Life Threatening Behavior*, *32*(2), 146-157.

Thompson, E.A., Mazza, J.J., Herting, J.R., Randell, B.P., and Eggert, L.L. (2005). The mediating roles of anxiety, depression, and hopelessness on adolescent suicidal behaviors. *Suicide and Life-Threatening Behavior*, *35*(1), 14-34.

Yoder, K.A. & Hoyt, D.R. (2005). Family economic pressure and adolescent suicidal behavior: Application of the Family Stress Model. *Suicide and Life-Threatening Behavior*, *35*(3), 251-264.

Elder suicide references

Adamek, M.E. & Kaplan, M.S. (1996). Managing elder suicide: A profile of American and Canadian crisis prevention centers. *Suicide and Life Threatening Behavior*, *26*(2), 122-131.

Conwell, Y. (2001). Suicide in later life: A review and recommendations for prevention. *Suicide and Life Threatening Behavior*, *31* (Suppl. 1), 6-31.

Haight, B.K. & Hendrix, S.A. (1998). Suicidal intent/life satisfaction: Comparing the life stories of older women. *Suicide and Life Threatening Behavior*, *28*(3), 272-284.

McIntosh, J. (1995). Suicide prevention in the elderly. *Suicide and Life Threatening Behavior*, *25*(1), 180-192.

Military suicide references

Moldeven, M. (1994). *Military-civilian teamwork in suicide prevention. Armed Forces' strategies, procedures, and responsibilities to implement their policy that suicide prevention is everybody's business.* Del Mar, CA: Moldeven Publishing.

Wong, A., Escobar, M., Lesage, A., Loyer, M., Vanier, C., & Sakinofsky, I. (2001). Are UN peacekeepers at risk for suicide? *Suicide and Life Threatening Behavior*, *31*(1), 103-112.

Corrections suicide references

Bonner, R.L. (2000). Correctional suicide prevention in the year 2000 and beyond. *Suicide and Life Threatening Behavior*, *30*(4), 370-376.

Fruehwald, S., Frottier, P., Eher, R. Gutierrez, K, & Ritter, K. (2000). Prison suicides in Austria. *Suicide and Life Threatening Behavior*, *30*(4), 360-369.

Web sites for helping agencies

American Red Cross. http://www.redcross.org.

Association of Traumatic Stress Specialists. http://www.atss-hq.com.

Compassionate Friends. http://www.compassionatefriends.org.

Concerns of Police Survivors. http://www.nationalcops.org.

David Baldwin's Trauma Pages. http://www.trauma-pages.org.

International Critical Incident Stress Foundation, Inc. http://www.icisf.org.

International Society for Traumatic Stress Studies. http://www.istss.org/.

National Center for PTSD. http://www.ncptsd.org.

National Institute on Alcohol Abuse and Alcoholism. http://www.niaaa.nih.gov.

National Insitute of Mental Health. http://www.nimh.nih.gov.

National Organization of Victim Assistance. http://www.try-nova.org.

Salvation Army. http://www.salvationarmy.org.

Substance Abuse and Mental Health Services. http://www.samhsa.gov/.

United Way. http://national.unitedway.org.

Web sites related to suicide

American Association of Suicidology. http://www.suicidology.org/.

American Foundation for Suicide Prevention. http://www.afsp.org/.

Befrienders Worldwide. http://www.befrienders.org/.

Canadian Association for Suicide Prevention. http://www.suicideprevention.ca/.

Depression and Bipolar Support Alliance. http://www.dbsalliance.org/

Healing for Survivors of Suicide. http://www.survivingsuicide.com/.

John L. McIntosh, Ph.D. HomePage. http://www.iusb.edu/~jmcintos/.

Living Works, Education, Inc. http://www.livingworks.net/.

National Organization for People of Color Against Suicide. http://www.nopcas.org/.

National Strategy for Suicide Prevention. http://www.mentalhealth.org/suicideprevention/.

National Suicide Prevention Resource Center. http://www.sprc.org/.

Organization for Attempters and Survivors of Suicide in Interfaith Services. http://www.oassis.org/.

Suicide Prevention Action Network USA, Inc. http://www.spanusa.org/.

Suicide Information & Education Centre. http://www.suicideinfo.ca/.

Survivors of a Loved One's Suicide. http://www.1000deaths.com/SOLOS.

Survivors of Suicide. http://www.survivorsofsuicide.com/.

Training Institute for Suicide Assessment & Clinical Interviewing. http://www.suicideassessment.com/.

U.S. Air Force Suicide Prevention Program. http://afspp.afms.mil/.

U.S. Army Suicide Prevention Resource Manual. http://hooah4health.com/toolbox/suicide/default.htm

U.S. Marine Corps Suicide Prevention. http://www.usmc-mccs.org/suicideprevent/index.cfm/.

U.S. Navy Suicide Prevention. http://www-nehc.med.navy.mil/hp/suicide/index.htm/.

Yellow Ribbon Suicide Prevention Program. http://www.yellowribbon.org/.

Exploring Law Enforcement Suicide: An Inside Look

2000 A.A.S Conference

Los Angeles, CA

Daniel W. Clark, Ph.D. & Elizabeth K. White, Ph.D.

This year, 134 new names will be added to the Law Enforcement Officers Memorial. However, an estimated 300 law enforcement suicides occur every year. Is it true that over twice as many law enforcement officers will die by their own hand as are killed in the line of duty?

We identified 25 research studies regarding police suicide. Fourteen of those studies provided enough information to compare suicide rates. Twelve studies showed law enforcement (LE) suicide rates exceeded both the general population and age/gender matched group rates.

However, Aamodt & Warlike conducted a meta-analysis of published suicide rates and concluded law enforcement officers (LEOs) are less likely to commit suicide than an age, gender, and race matched population. Five of the 25 studies showed that an officer is more likely to die by suicide than by homicide.

Why the discrepancy in LE suicide rates? First, consider the statement that the LE suicide rate is 2-3 times as high as the general population. Our population of LEOs does not mirror the "general population" from gender, age, or ethnic aspects. A more appropriate comparison group for LEOs is white males. If we compare the rate calculated by Aamodt & Warlike of 18.1/100,000 with the white male rate of 20.2, the rates are not nearly as different.

Second, the majority of studies involved large departments/cities with an occasional statewide study. National LE suicide rates are then extrapolated from these populations, which may not be representative of the occupation.

Third, the law enforcement culture works against accurate research and assessment.

Why do LEOs choose to commit suicide? Police suicide has been associated with relationship problems, shift work, criminal justice inconsistencies, alcohol and substance abuse, administration problems, a negative public image, and ready access to and familiarity with a firearm. LEOs may hold unrealistically high expectations. Some choose suicide to escape an intolerable situation.

Another factor is near-constant exposure to human suffering. LEOs tend to deal with other people's problems and see more "bad stuff" in the first years of their career than most people see in a lifetime.

Several suicidal risk factors have particular relevance within the police culture. LEOs choose their firearm as a suicide method an average of 86% compared to the national average of 59%. The officer has constant access to this highly lethal means. In addition, the average officer owns a back up weapon and perhaps additional weapons.

LEOs also have a second, very attractive means of suicide. When an officer dies in the line of duty, the family receives significant financial compensation. It is a heros death and the fallen officer is given highest honors. This can be a tempting way out for an officer. The clinician must be aware of such alternative methods of suicide as "suicide by suspect."

Alcohol abuse is an ongoing problem among the LE population. In a summary of nine studies on LE suicide and alcohol, 35% of the officer's suicides involved alcohol.

Although LEOs have greater solidarity than most other populations, this solidarity may not lend itself to sharing emotional or psychological concerns with peers. Social support may appear plentiful but be actually non-existent.

Police internal investigations are lengthy and can cause extreme anxiety. The threat of termination is very powerful because law enforcement is not something most LEOs do for a living. It is something they are!

Dealing with LE personnel in a clinical setting requires that the clinician have significant understanding of the world of law enforcement. It is essential that a clinician understand how a LEO presents in treatment and how that treatment should be handled.

Despite recent progress, LEOs still have reservations about entering treatment. They underutilize counseling services and often wait until the problems are well developed and entrenched before seeking treatment. LEOs are very concerned about job security and confidentiality. The officer may be relieved of duty and/or sent for a fitness for duty evaluation. Occasionally the officer is relieved of duty, then assigned to the same work location as a civilian, resulting in significant embarrassment and lack of privacy.

When a LEO is involved in a critical incident, the involved person(s) often sues. Counseling records are highly desirable data in this battle. Technically such records are protected but a judge often decides if these materials are admitted. Although California state law has recognized patient privilege for years, federal protection was established fairly recently. This may be particularly pertinent for LEOs, who often face federal allegations such as denial of civil rights.

Several common interventions are problematic when the client is a LEO. A clinician may recommend an individual obtain time off work. If a LEO is too "ill" to work, however, s/he has cast doubt on whether or not s/he is "fit for duty." If at all possible, the individual should obtain time off using other methods.

Second, LEOs are traditionally very leery of medications for fear of failing a urinalysis or concern that medication will impair their job performance. A clinician who wishes to use medication must take extra time to educate the officer about psychotropic medications and side effects, must be knowledgable about drug testing, and respectfully guide prescribing clinicians in their medication choice.

Clinicians may attempt to remove or control the means of potential suicide as a safety intervention. For a LEO, that means holding a firearm(s). However, who will adequately secure the weapon amidst the issues of privacy, reputation and job threat? Also, an officer without a firearm cannot work.

A final, drastic intervention is to involuntarily hospitalize the officer. However, the LEO is then at risk for significant job impact in terms of damaged reputation, being relieved of duty, and promotion or speciality assignment consideration.

In addition, per California law, anyone involuntarily hospitalized for risk to self may not carry or purchase a firearm for five years. An involuntary hospitalization means the officer may be terminated from current employment and will be unable to work in law enforcement for five years. In all honesty, short of a court appeal, the peace officer's career has ended.

In conclusion, remember that law enforcement personnel are generally a high functioning population. When they are at risk, they are at high risk. But when the crisis is past, they compensate quickly and often swiftly return to optimal functioning. It is essential that the clinician treating law enforcement personnel understands both the increased risk and the treatment peculiarities related to working with potentially suicidal law enforcement officers.

Daniel W. Clark, Ph.D.
Washington State Patrol
(360) 586-8492
wsp-psych@att.net

Elizabeth K. White, Ph.D.
Los Angeles Sheriffs Department
(213) 738-3500
EKWhite@lasd.org